Guile NCurses Library

A catalogue record for this book is available from the Hong Kong Public Libraries.

Published in Hong Kong by Samurai Media Limited.

Email: info@samuraimedia.org

ISBN 978-988-8381-63-0

Short Contents

Table of Contents

1 Introduction

1.1 Authors, Copyright, and Declarations

Michael Gran assembled this book, but, wrote only small sections of text. Most of reference text of the curses library was taken directly from the documentation of ncurses itself and was modified to make it specific to this Guile binding. The ncurses library is maintained by Tom Dickey, and the manual pages in the library note that the Free Software Foundation holds the copyright.

I've put his name on the title page, because it would seem rude not to do so; however, one should not get the impression that he approves of the Guile Ncurses project or that he is involved with the Guile NCurses project, or, indeed, that he is even aware of it.

The license for the original ncurses documentation is as follows.

The tutorial for the curses library is adapted from the *ncurses Programming HowTo* by Pradeep Padala. It was modified by Michael Gran to make it specific to the Guile binding.

Again, I've put his name on the title page, because it would seem rude not to do so; however, one should not get the impression that he approves of the Guile Ncurses project or that he is involved with the Guile Ncurses project, or, again, that he is even aware of it.

That document holds the following license.

2 Components of a Curses Interface

The goal of Ncurses is to simplify the task of programming for character-cell terminals. A character-cell terminal is a combination of a display that shows text in a monospaced font and the keyboard and mouse that connect to it. These days, there are three common types of terminals. Actual hardware terminals, such as the DEC VT220 or the Boundless Technologies VT525, are dedicated thin clients that interact with a networked computer via a serial port. These are still somewhat common in legacy applications or industrial applications where computers would be too expensive or too fragile, but, they are rapidly becoming extinct. Second are the consoles of text-mode operating systems, such as the console of GNU/Linux when used without X/Windows or the command prompt of FreeDOS. The third type is the terminal emulation programs that some windowing systems have. The best known terminal emulation program is probably XTerm, which does a good emulation of a VT220 terminal.

The Ncurses library attempts to create a standardized solution for these problems.

- A program needs to know which keys are pressed and when.
- A program needs to know a terminal's capabilities. Can text be bold, italic, or in color?
- A program needs to know how to exploit a terminal's capabilities. How does a program tell the terminal to move the cursor, to change text color, or to erase the screen?

2.1 Terminal Capabilities

The first step in any Ncurses program is to understand the terminal's capabilities and attributes. Ncurses includes a database of terminals and their capabilities called `terminfo` or perhaps `termcap`. When a Ncurses program is initialized, the type of terminal is queried, usually by examining the environment variable `TERM`, and the capabilities are read from the database.

2.2 Keyboards and Keys

When a key is pressed, one or more bytes are sent to the program by the keyboard driver. These bytes need to be converted by the program back into a key name. For ASCII characters, this conversion is trivial. A key press of *c* usually sends the ASCII encoding 142 (*c*) which can be understood to mean the letter "c". For other keys on the keypad, like F1 or HOME, the encoding can take multiple bytes and can differ from terminal to terminal. On some terminals, for example, pressing F1 is the same as if the user had typed *ESC O P*.

The `terminfo` database provides information that helps associate multibyte codes to keys on the keypad, and there are curses functions that will do the association.

2.3 Characters, Attributes, Colors, and Renditions

As the goal of curses is to allow a program to take advantage of the capabilities of terminal, each character on the screen has a *color pair* and a set of *attributes*.

In curses, the colors are usually defined in terms of *color pairs*, which is a combination of a foreground and a background color. Each character written to a terminal will have an associated color pair, assuming the terminal supports color.

Also each character has a set of attributes, such as *bold*, *underline*, or *blink*.

A character's color pair and its attributes are collectively called its *rendition*.

2.4 Windows

Curses uses the concept of a *window* to visually organize the terminal. A window is a rectangular area on the terminal. A terminal always has one default window which is the size of the physical screen. This may be further subdivided into other windows. The default window is called the *standard screen*.

Each window has a set of associated visual properties: the default rendition of characters added to it and whether it scrolls when text reaches the bottom of the screen, for example.

Each window forms a coordinate system for the display of characters. The top-left character location in the window is the origin, $(0, 0)$. x coordinates increase as one moves right and y coordinates increase as one moves down. Because the origin begins at zero, the largest allowable x value will be the number of columns minus one.

3 Types and encodings

Curses has several types specific to how it operates: rendered strings and windows, for example. Some of the curses types are represented by standard scheme types, while others are represented as opaque types (SMOBs).

3.1 Character types

The Guile Ncurses library uses two basic character types, simple characters and complex characters. Simple characters are the native Guile characters, and complex characters are those used to interact with the NCurses library. When using this library, a programmer will often have to convert simple characters to complex characters and vice versa, so it is important to understand their differences and applications.

Simple characters are the Guile native character type.

For older versions of Guile, such as the 1.6.x and the 1.8.x versions, characters were limited to being 8-bit. The lower 128 characters were ASCII, and the upper 128 characters had a meaning based on the locale of the system. If the locale were set to ISO-8859-1, for example, the upper 128 characters would be common accented letters used in western European languages. In almost all cases, each character took up the same space on a character cell terminal.

In newer versions of Guile, such as 2.0.x, the native Guile character type is a Unicode codepoint, a 32-bit number. Characters based on Unicode include all or most of the glyphs for the most languages. There are challenges when using the non-ASCII characters. There are double-width characters, such as hiragana and katakana, that take up two character spaces on a character cell terminal because of their complexity. There are combining characters, such as accents, that aren't intended to stand alone and actually modify the previous character in a string.

In the terminology of Unicode, a 32-bit integer that maps to a wide character is a *code point*, and documents that refer to Unicode code points typically write them like this: U+XXXX, where XXXX is a four-digit hexadecimal number.

simple characters

>An simple character is a standard Guile character, such as #\x. It is also referred to as an unrendered characters. It is *unrendered* because it has no associated color or attributes.

simple strings

>A simple string, also called an unrendered string, is a standard Guile string, such as "hello", which is a sequence of unrendered characters.

complex characters

>Rendered, complex characters usually are a standard character, zero to three combining characters, attribute information, and color information. The *attribute information* describes if the character is bold, dim, reverse video, etc. The guile ncurses library defines a special record type for complex characters: the *xchar*.

>Each complex character may contain more than one simple character. The first character in the list should be a base character or a control character. A base

character is usually a character than can be printed standalone: combining accents and other letter codepoints intended to modify another letter are not base characters. The remaining characters in the list, if any, are accents or other combining characters that modify the appearance of the base character. If the first character was a control character, no combining characters are allowed.

Here are examples of the constructors used to make complex characters. These constructors will be described in more detail later on.

```
;; A constructor for a letter 'x' using the default colors
> (normal #\x)

;; The display format of the resulting complex character
==> #<xchar #\x>

;; A constructor for a bold letter 'L' using default colors
> (bold #\L)

;; The display format of the resulting bold 'L' character
==> #<xchar bold #\L>

;; A bold letter 'x' printed white on a green background
> (init-pair! 2 COLOR_WHITE COLOR_GREEN)
> (bold-on (color 2 #\x))
==> #<xchar bold color-pair #2 [white on green] #\x>

;; A letter 'n' overwritten with a tilde
> (define ntilde (normal #\n))
> (set-xchar-chars! ntilde '(#\n #\~))
> ntilde
==> #<xchar #\n #\~>
```

rendered, complex strings

Rendered, complex strings are lists of rendered, complex characters.

An example of the constructor for a rendered complex string, and the display format of that string

```
;; The constructor for a complex string: the word 'hello' in
;; reverse video
> (inverse "hello")

;; The display format of the resulting string could be...
==> (#<xchar reverse color-pair #0 [white on black] #\h>
     #<xchar reverse color-pair #0 [white on black] #\e>
     #<xchar reverse color-pair #0 [white on black] #\l>
     #<xchar reverse color-pair #0 [white on black] #\l>
     #<xchar reverse color-pair #0 [white on black] #\o>)
```

3.2 Opaque types

These are types from system libraries that are complex or system-dependent. They are implemented as SMOBs.

The #<window> type

> The #<window> type is an opaque type that contains information about the characters and renditions for a given window. It is created by the function **newwin** and is used and most curses functions.

The #<screen> type

> The #<screen> type is an opaque types that contain information about the physical terminal. Variables of type #<screen> are created with the function **newterm** and used by the function **set-term**.
>
> This type is usually only found in programs that use multiple terminals.

The #<panel> type

> The #<panel> type is an opaque type that represents a window's place in a stack of windows. It is created with **new-panel**. It is used in functions that deal with overlapping windows

The #<item> type

> The #<item> type is an opaque type that represents one menu item in a menu. It is created with **new-item**. It is part of the menu library.

The #<menu> type

> The #<menu> type is an opaque type that represents a menu. It is created with **new-menu** from a list of #<item> types.

The #<field> type

> The #<field> type is an opaque type that represents one text box or entry on a form.

The #<form> type

> This represents a form, created using **new-form** from a list of elements of type #<field>.

4 Curses Tutorial

4.1 Hello World!!!

Welcome to the world of curses. Before we plunge into the library and look into its various features, let's write a simple program and say hello to the world.

4.1.1 Using the Guile Curses module

To use ncurses library functions, you have to load the (ncurses curses) module into the program.

Here is the Hello World program.

```
#!/usr/bin/guile
!#
(use-modules (ncurses curses))

(define stdscr (initscr))
(addstr stdscr "Hello World!!!")
(refresh stdscr)
(getch stdscr)
(endwin)
```

The first line of the example, #!/usr/bin/guile, gives the location of where Guile is installed on my system. This may differ on your system.

The above program prints "Hello World!!!" to the screen, waits for the user to press any key, and then exits. This program shows how to initialize curses and do screen manipulation and end curses mode. Let's dissect it line by line.

4.1.1.1 About initscr

The procedure initscr initializes the terminal in curses mode. It clears the screen and presents a blank screen. To do any screen manipulation using the curses package, this has to be called first. This function initializes the curses system and allocates memory for screen handling and some other data structures. It returns a SMOB that represents the default window: the window that represents the entire screen. By convention, this window is denoted stdscr, the *standard screen*. Under extreme cases, this function might fail due to insufficient memory to allocate memory for curses library's data structures.

The procedure initscr returns a #<window> that contains necessary information about the curses screen. The #<window> that is returned must be stored until the program is finished with the curses library. If that #<window> is garbage collected, the curses library cannot continue.

After this is done, we can do a variety of initializations to customize our curses settings

4.1.1.2 The mysterious refresh

The next line addstr prints the string "Hello World!!!" on to the screen. This function prints the data on a window called stdscr at the current (y, x) coordinates. Since our present coordinates are at 0,0 the string is printed at the top, left-hand corner of the window.

This brings us to the mysterious (refresh stdscr). Well, when we called addstr, the data is actually written to an imaginary window, which is not updated on the screen yet. The job of addstr is to update a few flags and data structures and write the data to a buffer corresponding to stdscr. In order to show it on the screen, we need to call refresh and tell the curses system to dump the contents on the screen.

The philosophy behind all this is to allow the programmer to do multiple updates on the imaginary screen or windows and to do a refresh once all the screen update is done. refresh checks the window and updates only the portion which has been changed. This improves performance and offers greater flexibility, too. But, it is sometimes frustrating to beginners. A common mistake committed by beginners is to forget to call refresh after they did some update through addstr.

4.1.1.3 About endwin

And finally, don't forget to end the curses mode. Otherwise your terminal might behave strangely after the program quits. endwin frees the memory taken by the curses sub-system and its data structures and puts the terminal in normal mode. This function must be called after you are done with curses mode.

4.2 Interactive sessions and guile-ncurses-shell

If you would like to try out these functions interactively by typing them into the scheme shell, instead of typing them and running them as scripts, the program guile-ncurses-shell can be used. The problem with interactive Guile sessions using curses is that you are typing into the same screen that curses is trying to manage, which leads to confusing results. The program guile-ncurses-shell, which must be run on X, starts an interactive guile session and creates and xterm that will be managed by curses. The results of the curses function calls will appear in the xterm, instead of in the screen where the interactive guile session occurs.

Here we'll try four functions: initscr sets up the screen, addstr writes a string to the screen, refresh redraws the screen, and endwin frees the screen.

Upon initialization guile-ncurses-shell automatically calls these functions.

```
(use-modules (ncurses curses))
(define %guile-ncurses-shell-stdscr (initscr))
```

It loads the ncurses module; initializes the screen; and saves the returned ncurses screen structure in the variable %guile-ncurses-shell-stdscr. Thus, you do not need to call (initscr) in your interactive session when you use guile-ncurses-shell.

The first thing you want to do is to redefine the name of the standard window to something more reasonable.

```
(define win %guile-ncurses-shell-stdscr)
```

To check and see if the guile-ncurses-shell is working, you can write a string onto the created xterm.

```
(addstr win "hello, world!")
(refresh win)
```

The guile-ncurses-shell communicates with the xterm using a read port and a write port. If, for some obscure reason, you need to access the read or write port directly, they are stored in the variables `%guile-ncurses-shell-read-port` and `%guile-ncurses-shell-write-port`.

When exiting an interactive session, by *C-D* for example, `guile-ncurses-shell` automatically calls (`endwin`), so you do not need to call that yourself.

4.3 The Gory Details

Now that we've seen how to write a simple curses program, let's get into the details. There are many functions that help customize what you see on the screen and many features which can be put to full use.

Here we go...

4.4 Initialization

We now know that to initialize curses the function `initscr` has to be called. There are functions which can be called after this initialization to customize our curses session. We may ask the curses system to set the terminal in raw mode or initialize color or initialize the mouse, etc. Let's discuss some of the functions that are normally called immediately after `initscr`.

4.4.1 Initialization Functions

4.4.1.1 `raw!` and `cbreak!`

Normally the terminal driver buffers the characters a user types until a newline or carriage return is encountered. But most programs require that the characters be available as soon as the user types them. The functions `cbreak!` and `raw!` are used to disable line buffering. The difference between these two functions is in the way control characters like suspend (*Ctrl-Z*), interrupt and quit (*Ctrl-C*) are passed to the program. In the `raw!` mode, these characters are directly passed to the program without generating a signal. In the `cbreak!` mode, these control characters are interpreted as any other character by the terminal driver, allowing *Ctrl-C* and *Ctrl-Z* to quit and suspend the program.

4.4.1.2 `echo!` and `noecho!`

These functions control the echoing of characters typed by the user to the terminal. `noecho!` switches off echoing. With echoing off, when a user presses a character, it is not displayed on the screen.

4.4.1.3 keypad!

This function enables the reading of function keys like F1, F2, arrow keys, etc. Almost every interactive program enables this, as arrow keys are a major part of any user interface. Do (`keypad! stdscr #t`) to enable this feature for the regular screen `stdscr` (assuming that `stdscr` is the variable you used to hold the output of `initscr`.)

4.4.1.4 halfdelay!

This function is useful when you want to ask the user for input, and if he doesn't respond within a certain time, do something else. One possible example would be a timeout at a password prompt. `halfdelay!` enables half-delay mode, which is similar to `cbreak!` mode in that characters types are immediately available to the program. However, after a period of time if there is no input, it returns #f.

4.4.2 An example

Let's write a program that will clarify the usage of these functions.

```
#!/usr/bin/guile
!#
(use-modules (ncurses curses))

(define stdscr (initscr))        ; Start curses mode
(raw!)                                               ; Line buf:
(keypad! stdscr #t)              ; We get F1, F2, etc
(noecho!)                                            ; Don't echo ۱
(addstr stdscr "Type any character to see it in bold\n")
(let ((ch (getch stdscr)))       ; Read a key press, put it in 'ch'
  (addstr stdscr "The pressed key is ")

  (if (char? ch)                 ; If a non-function key is pressed
      (addch stdscr (bold ch))   ; print its name

      (addchstr stdscr (bold (keyname ch)))) ; Or, print the function
                                 ; key name

  (refresh stdscr)              ; Print it on the real screen
  (getch stdscr)                ; Wait for user input
  (endwin))                     ; End curses mode
```

Hopefully this program is easy to follow even though I used functions that aren't explained yet. The procedure getch is used to get a character from the user. If it returns a character, the user pressed a character key. If it returns a number, the use pressed a function key. The (bold ch) adds the bold attribute to the character, and addch prints the character on the screen.

4.5 A word about windows

Before we plunge into the myriad ncurses functions, let me clear a few things about windows. Windows are explained in detail in the following sections.

A window is an imaginary screen defined by the curses system. A window does not mean a bordered window which you usually see in GNOME or KDE system. When curses is initialized, it creates a default window conventionally named stdscr which represents your 80x25 (or the size of window in which you are running) screen. If you are doing simple tasks like printing a few strings, reading input, etc., you can safely use this single window for all of your purposes. You can also create windows and call functions which explicitly work on the specified window.

For example, if you call

```
(addstr stdscr "Hi There!!!")
(refresh stdscr)
```

It prints the string on `stdscr` at the present cursor position. Similarly, the call to `refresh` works on `stdscr` only.

Say you have created multiple windows, then you have to call the functions separately on each window. When you call `refresh`, you need to call it on the window that was updated.

```
(addstr win "Hi There!!!")
(refresh win)
```

For many functions, there are optional key parameters.

```
(addstr stdscr string)               ; Print on stdscr at present
                                      ; cursor location
(addstr stdscr string #:y y #:x x)   ; Move to (y, x) then print string
```

4.6 Output functions

I guess you can't wait any more to see some action. Back to our odyssey of curses functions. Now that curses is initialized, let's interact with the world.

There are three primary functions which you can use to output characters and strings to the screen.

1. `addch`: output rendered characters

2. `addstr`: output unrendered strings

3. `addchstr`: output rendered strings

4.6.1 The `addch` procedure

The `addch` function puts a single rendered character into the current cursor location and advances the position of the cursor. Attributes are explained in detail in later sections of the document. If a character is associated with an attribute (bold, reverse video, etc.), when curses prints the character, it is printed with that rendition.

In order to combine a character with some attributes, you have two options:

1. You can explicitly construct a rendered character by passing a simple character through the rendition functions for the desired attributes:

```
(bold #\x)
(blink-on (bold-on #\x))
(color 2 #\x)
```

2. By using functions like `attr-set!`, `attr-on!`, `attr-off!`, you can manipulate the current attributes of the given window. Once set, the characters printed in the window are associated with the attributes until it is turned off.

Additionally, curses provides some special characters for character-based graphics. You can draw tables, horizontal or vertical lines. Try looking for the procedures beginning with `acs-`.

4.6.1.1 Moving the cursor `addch`

The optional key parameters `#:y y #:x x` can be used to move the cursor to a given point, and then print. Thus the calls

```
(move stdscr row col)
(addch stdscr ch)
```

can be replaced by

```
(addch stdscr ch #:y row #:x col)
```

4.6.1.2 Complex characters and `addch`

There are really two version of the NCurses library: a standard version and a *wide* version. When `guile ncurses` was compiled, it was associated with either the standard version `libncurses` or the wide version `libncursesw`. The wide version has greater capability to print non-Latin characters than the standard version.

For every C function that operates on characters, there is a parallel function that operates on wide characters. The guile ncurses library hides all of that complexity, and presents the same API regardless of whether it used `libncurses` or `libncursew`.

At this point, a C programmer familiar with `ncurses` might be wondering how to call `add-wch` to print, for example, a Chinese character. The guile ncurses library abstracts both the C ncurses function `addch` and the C ncurses function `add-wch` as the Guile function `addch`.

So, if you version of Guile is capable of Unicode characters (such as Guile version 2.0.x), and if you version of NCurses is the wide version `libncursesw`, then you can use this library to print non-Latin characters.

First off, if you want to use wide characters, you need to call `(setlocale LC_ALL "")` before the call to `initscr`. The locale that is set must be an encoding that has greater than 8-bit characters, such as UTF-8. Also, you terminal must be capable of printing non-Latin characters.

Then, to add a rendered, complex character to the screen, use `addch` and friends as before

```
;; Bold U+041B Cyrillic Capital Letter El
(addch stdscr (bold #\Л))
```

4.6.2 `addstr` class of functions

These functions output entire strings to the screen.

They can be used effectively in conjunction with the `format` procedure from `(ice-9 format)`.

4.6.3 A simple `addstr` example

```
#!/usr/bin/guile
!#

(use-modules (ncurses curses)
             (srfi srfi-1))

(define stdscr (initscr))

(let* ((mesg "Just a string")
       (len (string-length mesg))
       (siz (getmaxyx stdscr))
       (row (first siz))
```

```
         (col (second siz)))

;; Print the message centered in the window
(move stdscr
      (round (/ row 2))
      (round (/ (- col len) 2)))
(addstr stdscr mesg)

;; Use "format" to generate a message, and then print it
(addstr stdscr
        (format #f "This screen has ~a rows and ~a columns ~%"
                row col)
        #:y (- row 2)
        #:x 0)

(addstr stdscr "Try resizing your window (if possible) ")
(addstr stdscr "and then run this program again")
(refresh stdscr)

;; Wait for a keypress
(getch stdscr)
(endwin))
```

The above program demonstrates how easy it is to combine `addstr` and `move` to print at a specific location on the screen. It also shows how to use the equivalent key parameters `#:y` and `#:x`. They do exactly the same thing. It also shows how (`format #f ...`) can be used in conjunction with `addstr` to do formatted output.

The example introduces the new function `getmaxyx`. It gives the number of columns and the number of rows in a given window. `getmaxyx` does this by returning a list of two elements, `y` and `x`.

4.6.4 A word about coordinates

The `move` function takes the `y` coordinate first and then `x` as its arguments. A common mistake by beginners is to pass `x`, `y` in that order.

If you use the `#:y` and `#:x` key parameters that most output procedures have in lieu of using the `move` statement, you can use enter the coordinates in whichever order seems most natural to you.

```
;; either
(addstr win "Hi" #:x 0 #:y 10)
;; or
(addstr win "Hi" #:y 10 #:x 0)
```

4.7 Input functions

Well, printing without taking input is boring. Let's see functions which allow us to get input from the user.

1. `getch`: get a character

2. `getnstr`: get a string

4.7.1 `getch`

The procedure `getch` reads a single character from the terminal. But there are several subtle facts to consider. For example, if you don't use the function `cbreak!`, curses will not read your input characters contiguously, but, will begin to read them only after `RET` has been pressed or after and `EOF` has been encountered. In order to avoid this, the `cbreak!` function must be used so that characters are immediately available to your program. Another widely used function is `noecho!`. As the name suggests, when this function is set (used), the characters that are keyed in by the user will not show up on the screen. The two functions `cbreak!` and `noecho!` are typical examples of key management.

4.7.2 `getnstr`

The `getnstr` procedure is used to get strings from the terminal. In essence, it performs the same task as would be achieved by a series of calls to `getch` until a `NL`, `CR`, or `EOF` is received. The resulting string of characters is returned. The procedure always takes a length parameter which is the maximum length of string that it will allow to be input.

4.7.3 An example of `getnstr` and `getch`

```
#!/usr/bin/guile
!#
(use-modules (ncurses curses)
             (ice-9 format))

(define stdscr (initscr))

(let* ((mesg "Enter a string:  ")
       (len (string-length mesg))
       (siz (getmaxyx stdscr))
       (row (car siz))
       (col (cadr siz)))
  (addstr stdscr mesg
          #:y (round (/ row 2))
          #:x 0)

(refresh stdscr)
(let ((str (getnstr stdscr 80)))
  (addstr stdscr
          (format #f "You entered:  ~s~%" str)
          #:y (- row 2)
          #:x 0)

  (getch stdscr)))

(endwin)
```

4.8 Attributes

Attributes can be used to print characters with some special effects. Attributes, when set prudently, can present information in an easy, understandable manner.

The following program takes a scheme file as input and prints the file with comments in bold. It does so by turning on the A_BOLD attribute using attr-on! when a semicolon is detected, and then turning of the A_BOLD attribute using attr-off! when a newline is detected. Have a look.

```
#!/usr/bin/guile
!#

(use-modules (ncurses curses)
             (ice-9 format))

;; A helper function that return the cursor's current row
(define (getrow win)
  (car (getyx win)))

;; The program should be passed a filename from the command line
(if (not (eqv? 2 (length (command-line))))
    (begin
      (format #t "Usage: ~a <scm file name>~%" (car (command-line)))
      (primitive-exit 1)))

(let* ((filename (cadr (command-line)))
       (fport (open-input-file filename))
       (stdscr (initscr)))

  ;; Read one char at a time from the file
  (let loop ((ch (read-char fport)))
    (if (not (eof-object? ch))
        (begin
          ;; Wait for a key press once a page
          ;; of text has been printed
          (if (eqv? (getrow stdscr) (- (lines) 1))
              (begin
                (addstr stdscr "<-Press any key->")
                (refresh stdscr)
                (getch stdscr)
                (clear stdscr)
                (move stdscr 0 0)))
          ;; Bold all text between a semicolon
          ;; and the end of a line
          (cond
           ((eqv? ch #\;)
            (attr-on! stdscr A_BOLD))
           ((eqv? ch #\nl)
```

```
             (attr-off!  stdscr A_BOLD)))
          (addch stdscr (normal ch))
          (refresh stdscr)
          (loop (read-char fport)))

        ;; Clean up and exit
        (begin
          (addstr stdscr "<-Press any key->")
          (refresh stdscr)
          (getch stdscr)
          (endwin)
          (close-input-port fport)))))
```

One important thing to note is that in this program, **addch** is always passed a normal, un-bolded, character. Note the line

```
          (addch stdscr (normal ch))
```

But yet, the character printed by **addch** may still appear as bold on the screen. This is because the character attributes passed to **addch** combine with the character attributes set by **attr-on!**. If **attr-on!** has set the window's default attributes to bold, that will merge with the attributes passed to **addch**.

The function also introduces the useful function **getyx**. It returns the coordinates of the present cursor as a list of two elements.

The above program is really a simple one which doesn't do much. Along these lines once could write a more useful program which reads a scheme file, parses it, and prints it in different colors.

4.8.1 The details

Let's get into more details of attributes. The functions **attr-on!**, **attr-off!**, **attr-set!**, and their sister functions **attr-get** etc., can be used to switch attributes on and off, get attributes, and produce a colorful display.

The functions **attr-on!** and **attr-off!** take a bit-mask of attributes and switch them on or off respectively. The following video attributes can be passed to these functions.

A_NORMAL   Normal display (no highlight)

A_STANDOUT
          Best highlighting mode of the terminal

A_UNDERLINE
          Underlining

A_REVERSE
          Reverse video

A_BLINK   Blinking

A_DIM   Half-bright

A_BOLD   Extra bright or bold

A_PROTECT
> Protected mode

A_INVIS   Invisible or blank mode

A_ALTCHARSET
> Alternate character set

A_CHARTEXT
> Bit-mask to extract a character

A_HORIZONTAL
> Unsupported for now and left for future use

A_LEFT   Unsupported for now and left for future use

A_LOW   Unsupported for now and left for future use

A_RIGHT   Unsupported for now and left for future use

A_TOP   Unsupported for now and left for future use

A_VERTICAL
> Unsupported for now and left for future use

(color-pair n)
> A procedure that returns the bit mask for a color-pair

Colors are explained in the next sections.

We can `logior` any number of attributes to get a combined effect. If you wanted the character in window `win` to have reverse video with blinking characters, you can use

```
(attr-on! win (logior A_REVERSE A_BLINK))
```

4.8.2 attr-on! vs attr-set!

Then what is the difference between `attr-on!` and `attr-set!`? `attr-set!` sets the attributes of a window whereas `attr-on!` just switches on the attribute given to it. So `attr-set!` fully overrides whatever attributes the window previously had and sets it to the new attribute(s). Similarly, `attr-off!` just switches off the attributes(s) given to it as an argument. This gives us the flexibility of managing attributes easily. But, if you use them carelessly, you may lose track of what attributes the window has and garble the display. This is especially true while managing menus with colors and highlighting. So decide on a consistent policy and stick to it. You can always use `standend!` which is equivalent to `(attr-set! win A_NORMAL)` which turns off all attributes and brings you back to normal mode.

4.8.3 attr-get

The function `attr-get` gets the current attributes and color pair of the window. Though we might not use this as often as the above functions, this is useful in scanning areas of a screen. Say we wanted to do some complex update on the screen and we are not sure what attribute each character is associated with. Then this function can be used with either `attr-set!` or `attr-on!` to produce the desired effect.

4.8.4 `chgat` function

The function `chgat`, which is short for *change attributes*, can be used to set attributes for a group of characters already on the screen without moving the cursor. It changes the attributes of a given number of characters starting at the current cursor location.

You can pass it -1 as the character count to update until the end of the current line.

The following example changes the attributes of characters from the current position to the end of the line to reverse video on a window named `win1`.

```
(chgat win1 -1 A_REVERSE 0)
```

The are optional key parameters `#:y` and `#:x` can be used with `chgat`.

The following example will print a string on the screen. Then it will set the first 5 characters of the string to blink and change color to cyan.

```
#!/usr/bin/guile
!#

(use-modules (ncurses curses))

(define stdscr (initscr))

;; Prep the color functions
(start-color!)

;; Label cyan on black as color-pair #1
(init-pair!  1 COLOR_CYAN COLOR_BLACK)

(addstr stdscr "Blink Don't Blink")

(chgat    stdscr              ; window
          5                   ; num of chars
          A_BLINK             ; attributes
          1                   ; use color pair #1
          #:y 0               ; start y
          #:x 0)              ; start x

;; Move the cursor out of the way
(move stdscr 1 0)

(refresh stdscr)
(getch stdscr)
(endwin)
```

This example also introduces us to the color world of curses. Colors will be explained in detail later. Use 0 for white on black.

Now wait... Did you try running this little script? Did it work? Blinking is one of those features that may not be implemented on your terminal. As of the moment of this writing, Gnome terminal doesn't do blinking. The standard xterm does do blinking, but, it doesn't blink at the location of the cursor.

4.9 Windows Tutorial

Windows form the most important concept in curses. You have seen the standard window `stdscr` used in most of the previous examples. Now to design even a simplest GUI, you need to resort to windows. The main reason you may want to use windows is to manipulate parts of the screen separately, for better efficiency, by updating only the windows that need to be changed, and for a better design. I would say the last reason is the most important in going for windows. You should always strive for a better and easy-to-manage design in your programs. If you are writing big, complex GUIs, this is of pivotal importance before you start doing anything.

Now, anyone that has worked with a modern GUI has an intuitive understanding of what a "window" is. You will need to unlearn this knowledge when programming curses windows.

First off, a curses window doesn't necessarily have any sort of border or decoration that separates it from the rest of the terminal. You can make a curses window and then draw a border on it, but, that is up to the programmer.

Second, curses windows don't normally overlap. They are usually distinct, non-overlapping regions of the screen.

4.9.1 The basics

A window can be created by calling the function `newwin`. It doesn't draw anything on the screen initially. It allocates memory for a structure to manipulate the window and updates the structure with data regarding the window, like it's size, position, etc.

The function `newwin`, like `initscr`, returns a `#<window>`. Just like the `stdscr` created by `initscr`, the window created by `newwin` can be used in any procedure that takes a window argument. The window returned by `newwin` needs to remain in scope for as long as the window is to be used. If it is garbage collected, the memory associated with the window will eventually be freed.

The memory associated with a window can be more quickly freed by explicitly calling `delwin`. It will deallocate the memory associated with the window structure. Any further attempts to then use that window will cause an error.

4.9.2 Let there be a window

What fun is it if a window is created and we can't see it? So the fun part begins by displaying the window. The functions `box` and `border` can be used to draw a border around the window. Let's explore these functions in more detail in this example.

This example isn't meant as a practical example of what windows are good for. It just shows how to make, draw, erase, and destroy them.

```
#!/usr/bin/guile
!#

(use-modules (ncurses curses))

;; This procedure makes a new window and draws a box
;; around it
(define (create-newwin height width starty startx)
```

```
  ((lambda (win)                          ; Make a lambda proc that
     (box win (acs-vline) (acs-hline))    ; Makes a box,
     (refresh win)                        ; Draws the window
     win)                                 ; Returns the window to the caller

   (newwin height width starty startx))) ; Create a window and apply it
                                          ; to the lambda function

;; This procedure erases the box around a window and then deletes it
(define (destroy-win win)
  (let ((s (normal #\sp)))
    (border win s s s s s s s s)         ; Draw a box of spaces
    (refresh win)
    (delwin win)))

;; This prodecure deletes a window than then draw a new one someplace
;; else
(define (move-win win height width starty startx)
  (destroy-win win)
  (create-newwin height width starty startx))


;; Program Begins
(define stdscr (initscr))                ; Start curses
(cbreak!)                                ; Line buffering disabled
(keypad!  stdscr #t)                     ; Check for function keys


(let* ((height 3)
       (width 10)
       (starty (round (/ (- (lines) height) 2)))
       (startx (round (/ (- (cols) width) 2))))

  (addstr stdscr "Press F1 to exit")
  (refresh stdscr)
  (let loop ((starty starty)
             (startx startx)
             (my-win (create-newwin height width starty startx))
             (ch (getch stdscr)))
    (cond
     ((eqv?  ch KEY_LEFT)
      (loop starty
            (- startx 1)
            (move-win my-win height width starty (- startx 1))
            (getch stdscr)))

     ((eqv?  ch KEY_RIGHT)
```

```
        (loop starty
              (+ startx 1)
              (move-win my-win height width starty (+ startx 1))
              (getch stdscr)))

        ((eqv? ch KEY_UP)
         (loop (- starty 1)
               startx
               (move-win my-win height width (- starty 1) startx)
               (getch stdscr)))

        ((eqv? ch KEY_DOWN)
         (loop (+ starty 1)
               startx
               (move-win my-win height width (+ starty 1) startx)
               (getch stdscr)))

        ((eqv? ch (key-f 1))
         #f)

        (else
         (loop starty startx my-win (getch stdscr)))))))

     (endwin))
```

Don't scream. I know it is a big example. But there are some important things to explain here. This program creates a rectangular window that can be moved with left, right, up, and down arrow keys. It repeatedly creates and destroys windows as a user presses a key. Don't go beyond the screen limits. Checking for limits is left as an exercise for the reader. Let's dissect it line by line.

The **create-newwin** function creates a window with **newwin** and draws a box around it with **box**. For the horizontal lines in the box, I chose the special drawing character **acs-hline**. The vertical lines are the special drawing character **acs-vline**. For the corners of the box, the **box** procedure will use a guess of the best available corners for the terminal.

Most terminals will have special box drawing characters available. The procedure **acs-hline** and **acs-vline** will return these special drawing characters. If the terminal you are using does not have box drawing characters available, **acs-hline** and **acs-vline** will return the hyphen "-" and the vertical bar "|".

The procedure **destroy-win** first erases the window from the screen by painting a border of blanks and then calling **delwin** to deallocate memory related to it. Depending on the key the user presses, **startx** and **starty** are changed, and a new window is created.

In the **destroy-win**, as you can see, I used **border** instead of **box**. The reason is this: **border** draws a border around the window and the characters given to it as the four corners and the four lines. To put it clearly, if you called border as below:

```
(border win
        (normal #\|)
```

```
(normal #\|)
(normal #\-)
(normal #\-)
(normal #\+)
(normal #\+)
(normal #\+)
(normal #\+))
```

it produces something like this

```
+-----+
|     |
|     |
|     |
+-----+
```

It wouldn't have been sufficient to use (box win (normal #\sp) (normal #\sp)) to erase the box, because the box procedure still would have drawn the four corners of the box.

4.9.3 Other functions

You can also see in the above examples that I have used the procedures cols, and lines. These procedures return the size of the stdscr.

The function getch as usual gets the key from the keyboard, and then the cond expression acts on the key pressed. This type of cond expression is very common in any GUI-based program.

4.9.4 Other border functions

The box and border procedures are useful, but, they only draw borders around the outside of windows. If you want to draw lines on the screen is other locations than the border of windows, you can use the hline and vline procedures.

The following little program shows how to draw a box at any location. To draw a box, it needs to draw four corners, two horizontal lines, and two vertical lines. It uses hline and vline. These two functions are simple. They create a horizontal or vertical line of the specified length at the specified position. The program uses more of the special drawing characters like (acs-urcorner), which is the upper-right corner of a box.

```
#!/usr/bin/guile
!#

(use-modules (ncurses curses))

(define stdscr (initscr))

;; Draw a box the hard way
(define (box2 win y x height width)
  ;; top
  (move win y x)
  (addch win (acs-ulcorner))
```

```
(move win y (1+ x))
(hline win (acs-hline) (- width 2))
(move win y (+ x width -1))
(addch win (acs-urcorner))

;; left side
(move win (+ y 1) x)
(vline win (acs-vline) (- height 2))

;; right side
(move win (+ y 1) (+ x width -1))
(vline win (acs-vline) (- height 2))

;; bottom
(move win (+ y height -1) x)
(addch win (acs-llcorner))
(move win (+ y height -1) (1+ x))
(hline win (acs-hline) (- width 2))
(move win (+ y height -1) (+ x width -1))
(addch win (acs-lrcorner)))

(let* ((stdscr (initscr))
       (height 3)
       (width 10)
       (y (round (/ (- (lines) height) 2)))
       (x (round (/ (- (cols) width) 2))))
  (box2 stdscr y x height width)
  (refresh stdscr)
  (sleep 3)
  (endwin))
```

4.10 Colors

4.10.1 The basics of color

Life seems dull with no colors. Curses has a nice mechanism to handle colors. Let's get into the thick of things with a small program.

```
#!/usr/bin/guile
!#
(use-modules (ncurses curses))

(define stdscr (initscr))
(if (has-colors?)
    (begin
      (start-color!)
      (init-pair!  1 COLOR_GREEN COLOR_YELLOW)
      (attr-on!  stdscr (logior A_BOLD (color-pair 1)))
```

```
        (addstr stdscr "Voila!!  In color...")
        (refresh stdscr)
        (sleep 3)
        (endwin)
        0)
    (begin
      (endwin)
      (display "Your terminal does not support color")
      1))
```

As you can see, to start using color, you should first call **start-color!**. After that you can use color capabilities of your terminal. To find out whether a terminal has color capabilities or not, you can use **has-colors?**, which returns **#f** if the terminal does not support color.

Curses initializes all the color support for the terminal when **start-color!** is called. Usually, a color terminal will have at least eight colors available that can be accessed by constants like **COLOR_BLACK**, etc. Now to actually start using colors, you have to define pairs. Colors are always used in pairs. That means you have to use the function **init-pair!** to define the foreground and background for the pair number you give. After that, that pair number can be used as a normal attribute with the **color-pair** procedure. This may seem to be cumbersome at first.

The following colors are defined. You can use these as parameters for the various color functions.

1. COLOR_BLACK
2. COLOR_RED
3. COLOR_GREEN
4. COLOR_YELLOW
5. COLOR_BLUE
6. COLOR_MAGENTA
7. COLOR_CYAN
8. COLOR_WHITE

4.10.2 Changing color definitions

Most terminals don't support defining new colors or changing the colors that already exist. For those terminals that do, the function **init-color!** can be used to change the definition of colors by adjusting the amount of red, green, and blue in each. To set the red to a darker red, you could use this function

```
;; Param 1: color name
;; Param 2, 3, 4; RGB content, min=0 max=1000
(init-color! COLOR_RED 300 0 0)
```

If your terminal cannot change the color definitions, the procedure will throw and error. The function **can-change-color?** can be used to find out whether that terminal has the capability of changing color content or not. The RGB content is scaled from 0 to 1000. Initially, red is likely defined with content 680 (r), 0 (g), 0 (b).

The functions `color-content` and `pair-content` can be used to find the color content of a given color and foreground/background combination of a color pair.

4.11 Interfacing with the keyboard

4.11.1 The basics of keys

No GUI is complete without a strong user interface and to interact with the user, a curses program should be sensitive to key presses or mouse actions done by the user. Let's deal with keys first.

As you have seen in almost all of the above examples, it's very easy to get key input from the user. A simple way of getting key presses is the `getch` procedure. The `cbreak!` mode should be enabled to read keys when you are interested in reading individual key hits rather than complete lines of text (which usually end with a `CR`). `keypad!` should be enabled to get the function keys, arrow keys and so on.

`getch` returns a character if the key pressed maps to a standard character or it returns an integer code for those keys that don't map to characters, such as `PAGE UP` or `DELETE`. This integer code which can be matched with the `KEY_` constants. For example, if the user presses `F1`, the integer returned is 265. The procedure `(key-f 1)` returns 265.

For example, if you call `getch` like this

```
(let ((x (getch win)))
  ...
```

`getch` will wait for the user to press a key, (unless you specified a timeout), and when the user presses a key, the corresponding character or integer is returned. If it is an integer, then you can check the value returned with the `KEY_` constants or the result of the function key procedure `key-f`.

The following code piece will do that job

```
(let ((ch (getch win)))
    (if (eqv? ch KEY_LEFT)
        (addstr win "Left arrow is pressed")))
```

Let's write a small program which creates a menu that can be navigated by up and down arrows.

4.11.2 A simple key usage example

```
#!/usr/bin/guile
!#

(use-modules (ncurses curses))

;; Draw the menu on to the window WIN, using the list of CHOICES,
;; highlighting the currently selected entry.
(define (print-menu win highlight choices)
  (let ((x 2)
        (y 2)
        (n-choices (length choices)))
```

```scheme
;; The menu border
(box win (acs-vline) (acs-hline))

;; The menu entries from CHOICES, with the current entry
;; highlighted
(let loop ((i 0)
           (y y)
           (n n-choices))

   (cond
    ((eqv? highlight i)
     (attr-on! win A_REVERSE)
     (move win y x)
     (addstr win (list-ref choices i))
     (attr-off! win A_REVERSE))
    (else
     (move win y x)
     (addstr win (list-ref choices i))))

   (if (< i (- n-choices 1))
       (loop (+ 1 i)
             (+ 1 y)
             n-choices)
       (refresh win)))))


;; This loop lets the user select a menu.  It returns the number of the
;; selected item.
(define (get-selection menu-win highlight choices)
  (let ((n-choices (length choices)))
    (let loop ((highlight highlight)
               (ch (getch menu-win)))

      (cond

        ((eqv? ch KEY_UP)
         ((lambda (h)
            (print-menu menu-win h choices)
            (loop h (getch menu-win)))
          (if (eqv? highlight 0)
              (- n-choices 1)
              (- highlight 1))))

        ((eqv? ch KEY_DOWN)
         ((lambda (h)
            (print-menu menu-win h choices)
```

```
           (loop h (getch menu-win)))
         (if (eqv?  highlight (- n-choices 1))
             0
             (+ highlight 1))))

       ;; If enter or return is pressed, return the current selected
       ;; menu item
       ((or (eqv?  ch #\nl) (eqv?  ch KEY_ENTER))
        highlight)

       (else
        (loop highlight (getch menu-win)))))))))


(define (main)
  (let ((stdscr(initscr)))
    (cbreak!)
    (noecho!)

    (let* ((menu-width 30)
           (menu-height 10)
           (startx (round (/ (- (cols) menu-width) 2)))
           (starty (round (/ (- (lines) menu-height) 2)))
           (menu-win (newwin menu-height menu-width starty startx))
           (choices '("Choice 1"
                      "Choice 2"
                      "Choice 3"
                      "Choice 4"
                      "Exit"))
           (highlight 0))
      (begin
        (keypad!  menu-win #t)
        (print-menu menu-win 0 choices)
        (let ((choice (get-selection menu-win highlight choices)))
          (move stdscr 23 0)
          (addstr stdscr (format #f "You chose ~s ~%"
                          (list-ref choices choice)))
          (clrtoeol stdscr)
          (refresh stdscr)
          (sleep 2)
          (endwin)
          0)))))


(main)
```

4.12 Interfacing with the mouse

Now that you have seen how to get keys, let's do the same thing from the mouse. Usually each UI allows the user to interact with both keyboard and mouse.

4.12.1 The basics of the mouse

Before you do anything else, the events you want to receive have to be enabled with `mousemask`. You pass it a bit mask of events you would like to listen. By default, all the events are turned off. The bit mask `ALL_MOUSE_EVENTS` can be used to get all the events.

For current technology, the following events are of use.

Name	Description
BUTTON1_PRESSED	mouse button 1 down
BUTTON1_RELEASED	mouse button 1 up
BUTTON1_CLICKED	mouse button 1 clicked
BUTTON1_DOUBLE_CLICKED	mouse button 1 double clicked
BUTTON2_PRESSED	mouse button 2 down
BUTTON2_RELEASED	mouse button 2 up
BUTTON2_CLICKED	mouse button 2 clicked
BUTTON2_DOUBLE_CLICKED	mouse button 2 double clicked
BUTTON_SHIFT	shift was down during button state change
BUTTON_CTRL	control was down during button state change
BUTTON_ALT	alt was down during button state change
ALL_MOUSE_EVENTS	report all button state changes
REPORT_MOUSE_POSITION	report mouse movement

There similar constants for mouse button #3 and #4.

There are some important things to note.

1. Mouse buttons 1, 2, and 3 may be right, center, and left respectively, instead of right, left, and center.

2. The `BUTTON_SHIFT`, `BUTTON_ALT`, and `BUTTON_CTRL` codes will probably not work, as they will probably be intercepted by the window manager.

3. The mouse driver will not send both a click/release pair and a pressed message.

4.12.2 Getting the events

Once a class of mouse events have been enabled, `getch` and friends return `KEY_MOUSE` every time some mouse event happens. Then, the mouse event can be retrieved with `getmouse`.

`getmouse` returns a list of five elements: id, x, y, z, and flags. The flags contain information about mouse button events.

Schematically, decoding mouse events could look like this. (Note that I've used some of the srfi-1 list functions in this example.)

```
(set! c (getch win))
(if (eqv? c KEY_MOUSE)
    (let* ((m (getmouse))
```

```
                    (mouse-x (second m))
                    (mouse-y (third m))
                    (mouse-flag (fifth m)))
                (cond
                 ((logtest BUTTON1_PRESSED mouse-flag)
                  ; do button1-pressed response here
                 )
                 ((logtest BUTTON1_RELEASED mouse-flag)
                  ; do button1-released response here
                 ))))
```

4.12.3 Miscellaneous functions

The function `mouse-trafo` can be used to convert mouse coordinates to screen relative coordinates.

The `mouseinterval` function sets the maximum time (in thousandths of a second) that can elapse between press and release events in order for them to be recognized as a click. The default is one-fifth of a second.

4.13 Panels Library

Curses was originally build around the idea of having tiled text windows, where they did not overlap. The API is not set up to do the bookkeeping for overlapping windows.

Now that you are proficient in curses, you wanted to do some thing big. You created a lot of overlapping windows to give a professional windows-type look. Unfortunately, it soon becomes difficult to manage these. The multiple refreshes, updates plunge you into a nightmare. The overlapping windows create blotches, whenever you forget to refresh the windows in the proper order.

Don't despair. There's an elegant solution provided in panels library.

When your interface design is such that windows may dive deeper into the visibility stack or pop to the top at runtime, the resulting book-keeping can be tedious and difficult to get right. Hence the panels library.

If you have lot of overlapping windows, then panels library is the way to go. It obviates the need of doing series of **noutrefresh**, **doupdate** and relieves the burden of doing it correctly (bottom up). The library maintains information about the order of windows, their overlapping and update the screen properly. So why wait? Let's take a close peek into panels.

4.13.1 Panels Basics

The `#<panel>` object is a window that is implicitly treated as part of a deck including all other panel objects. The deck is treated as a stack with the top panel being completely visible and the other panels may or may not be obscured according to their positions. So the basic idea is to create a stack of overlapping panels and use panels library to display them correctly. There is a function similar to **refresh** which, when called , displays panels in the correct order. Functions are provided to hide or show panels, move panels, change its size etc.. The overlapping problem is managed by the panels library during all the calls to these functions.

The general flow of a panel program goes like this:

1. Create the windows (with `newwin`) to be attached to the panels.

2. Create panels with the chosen visibility order. Stack them up according to the desired visibility. The function `new-panel` is used to create panels.

3. Call `update-panels` to write the panels to the virtual screen in correct visibility order. Do a `doupdate` to show it on the screen.

4. Manipulate the panels with `show-panel`, `hide-panel`, `move-panel` etc. Make use of helper functions like `panel-hidden` and `panel-window`.

5. When you are done with the panel use `del-panel` to delete the panel.

Let's make the concepts clear, with some programs. The following is a simple program which creates 3 overlapping panels and shows them on the screen.

4.13.2 Compiling With the Panels Library

To use panels library functions, you have to use the module (ncurses panel).

```
#!/usr/bin/guile
!#

(use-modules (ncurses curses)
             (ncurses panel))

(define stdscr (initscr))

(let* ((win1 (newwin 5 10 5 5))
       (win2 (newwin 5 10 7 7))
       (panel1 (new-panel win1))
       (panel2 (new-panel win2)))
  (box win1 (acs-vline) (acs-hline))
  (addstr win1 "box 1"  #:y 1 #:x 1)
  (box win2 (acs-vline) (acs-hline))
  (addstr win2 "box 2" #:y 1 #:x 1)
  (update-panels)
  (doupdate)
  (sleep 1)

  ;; Move panel 1 to the bottom
  (addstr win1 "bottom" #:y 1 #:x 1)
  (bottom-panel panel1)
  (update-panels)
  (doupdate)
  (sleep 1)

  ;; Move panel 1 to the top
  (addstr win1 "top    " #:y 1 #:x 1)
  (top-panel panel1)
  (update-panels)
```

```
(doupdate)
(sleep 1)

;; Hide panel 1
(addstr win1 "hide    " #:y 1 #:x 1)
(hide-panel panel1)
(update-panels)
(doupdate)
(sleep 1)

;; Unhide panel 1
(addstr win1 "show    " #:y 1 #:x 1)
(show-panel panel1)
(update-panels)
(doupdate)
(sleep 1)

;; Move panel 1
(addstr win1 "move    " #:y 1 #:x 1)
(move-panel panel1 2 2)
(update-panels)
(doupdate)
(sleep 1))

(endwin)
```

As you can see, above program follows a simple flow. The windows are created with **newwin** and then they are attached to panels with **new-panel**. As we attach one panel after another, the stack of panels gets updated. To put them on screen **update-panels** and **doupdate** are called.

The panels can be brought to the front with **top-panel** or pushed to the back with **bottom-panel**. They can be removed with **hide-panel**, and then unhidden with **show-panel**.

4.13.3 Moving and Resizing Panels

The procedure **move-panel** can be used to move a panel to the desired location. It does not change the position of the panel in the stack. Make sure that you use **move-panel** instead **mvwin** on the window associated with the panel.

Resizing a panel is slightly complex. There is no straight forward function just to resize the window associated with a panel. A solution to resize a panel is to create a new window with the desired sizes, change the window associated with the panel using **replace-panel!**. Don't forget to delete the old window. The window associated with a panel can be found by using the function **panel-window**.

4.14 Menu Library

The menus library provides a nice extension to basic curses, through which you can create menus. It provides a set of functions to create menus. But they have to be customized to give a nicer look, with colors etc. Let's get into the details.

A menu is a screen display that assists the user to choose some subset of a given set of items. To put it simple, a menu is a collection of items from which one or more items can be chosen. Some readers might not be aware of multiple item selection capability. The menu library provides functionality to write menus from which the user can chose more than one item as the preferred choice. This is dealt with in a later section. Now it is time for some rudiments.

4.14.1 Menu basics

To create menus, you first create items, and then post the menu to the display. After that, all the processing of user responses is done in an elegant function `menu-driver` which is the work horse of any menu program.

The general flow of control of a menu program looks like this.

1. Initialize curses

2. Create items using `new-item`. You can specify a name and description for the items.

3. Create the menu with `new-menu` by specifying the items with which it is to be attached.

4. Post the menu with `menu-post` and refresh the screen.

5. Process the user requests with a loop and do necessary updates to menu with `menu-driver`.

6. Unpost the menu with `menu-unpost`.

7. End curses.

Let's see a program which prints a simple menu and updates the current selection with up, down arrows.

To use menu library functions, you have to use the module `(ncurses menu)`.

```
#!/usr/local/bin/guile
-s
!#

(use-modules (srfi srfi-1)
             (ncurses curses)
             (ncurses menu))

(define stdscr (initscr))
(cbreak!)
(noecho!)
(keypad! stdscr #t)

(let* (;; Labels for the menu items
       (names '("Choice 1" "Choice 2" "Choice 3" "Choice 4" "Exit"))
       (descriptions '("Description 1" "Description 2" "Description 3"
```

```
                          "Description 4" ""))

      ;; Create menu items for each label
      (my-items (map (lambda (name desc) (new-item name desc))
                     names
                     descriptions))
      ;; Create the menu
      (my-menu (new-menu my-items)))

;; Draw the menu
(move stdscr (- (lines) 2) 0)
(addstr stdscr "Press 'q' to Quit")
(post-menu my-menu)
(refresh stdscr)

;; Process the up and down arrow keys.  Break the loop if F1 is
;; pressed.  Ignore other keys.
(let loop ((c (getch stdscr)))
  (cond

    ;; Move down the menu when down arrow is pressed and then loop.
    ((eqv? c KEY_DOWN)
     (begin
       (menu-driver my-menu REQ_DOWN_ITEM)
       (loop (getch stdscr))))

    ;; Move up the menu when the up arrow is pressed and then loop.
    ((eqv? c KEY_UP)
     (begin
       (menu-driver my-menu REQ_UP_ITEM)
       (loop (getch stdscr))))

    ;; When enter is pressed, return the selection and quit.
    ((or (eqv? c KEY_ENTER)
         (eqv? c #\cr)
         (eqv? c #\nl))
     (begin
       (unpost-menu my-menu)
       (move stdscr (- (lines) 4) 0)
       (addstr stdscr
               (format #f "You selected item #~a: ~a"
                       (item-index (current-item my-menu))
                       (item-name (current-item my-menu))))
       (refresh stdscr)
       (sleep 2)))

    ;; If 'Q' or 'q'  is pressed, quit.  Otherwise, loop.
```

```
((not (or (eqv? c #\Q) (eqv? c #\q)))
(loop (getch stdscr)))))

(endwin))
```

This program demonstrates the basic concepts involved in creating a menu using menus library. First we create the items using **new-item** and then attach them to the menu with **new-menu** function. After posting the menu and refreshing the screen, the main processing loop starts. It reads user input and takes corresponding action. The function **menu-driver** is the main work horse of the menu system. The second parameter to this function tells what's to be done with the menu. According to the parameter, **menu-driver** does the corresponding task. The value can be either a menu navigational request, an ASCII character, or a KEY_MOUSE special key associated with a mouse event.

The menu_driver accepts following navigational requests.

REQ_LEFT_ITEM
> Move left to an item.

REQ_RIGHT_ITEM
> Move right to an item.

REQ_UP_ITEM
> Move up to an item.

REQ_DOWN_ITEM
> Move down to an item.

REQ_SCR_ULINE
> Scroll up a line.

REQ_SCR_DLINE
> Scroll down a line.

REQ_SCR_DPAGE
> Scroll down a page.

REQ_SCR_UPAGE
> Scroll up a page.

REQ_FIRST_ITEM
> Move to the first item.

REQ_LAST_ITEM
> Move to the last item.

REQ_NEXT_ITEM
> Move to the next item.

REQ_PREV_ITEM
> Move to the previous item.

REQ_TOGGLE_ITEM
> Select/deselect an item.

REQ_CLEAR_PATTERN
> Clear the menu pattern buffer.

`REQ_BACK_PATTERN`
>   Delete the previous character from the pattern buffer.

`REQ_NEXT_MATCH`
>   Move to the next item matching the pattern match.

`REQ_PREV_MATCH`
>   Move to the previous item matching the pattern match.

Don't get overwhelmed by the number of options. We will see them slowly one after another. The options of interest in this example are `REQ_UP_ITEM` and `REQ_DOWN_ITEM`. These two options when passed to menu_driver, menu driver updates the current item to one item up or down respectively.

4.14.2 Menu Driver: The work horse of the menu system

As you have seen in the above example, `menu-driver` plays an important role in updating the menu. It is very important to understand various options it takes and what they do. As explained above, the second parameter to `menu-driver` can be either a navigational request, a printable character or a `KEY_MOUSE` key. Let's dissect the different navigational requests.

`REQ_LEFT_ITEM` and `REQ_RIGHT_ITEM`
>   A menu can be displayed with multiple columns for more than one item. This can be done by using the `menu-format` function. When a multicolumnar menu is displayed these requests cause the menu driver to move the current selection to left or right.

`REQ_UP_ITEM` and `REQ_DOWN_ITEM`
>   These two options you have seen in the above example. These options when given, makes the `menu-driver` to move the current selection to an item up or down.

`REQ_SCR_*` options
>   The four options `REQ_SCR_ULINE`, `REQ_SCR_DLINE`, `REQ_SCR_DPAGE`, `REQ_SCR_UPAGE` are related to scrolling. If all the items in the menu cannot be displayed in the menu sub window, then the menu is scrollable. These requests can be given to the `menu-driver` to do the scrolling either one line up, down or one page down or up respectively.

`REQ_FIRST_ITEM`, `REQ_LAST_ITEM`, `REQ_NEXT_ITEM` and `REQ_PREV_ITEM`
>   Easy enough.

`REQ_TOGGLE_ITEM`
>   This request when given, toggles the present selection. This option is to be used only in a multivalued menu. So to use this request the option `O_ONEVALUE` must be off. This option can be made off or on with `set_menu_opts`.

`Pattern Requests`
>   Every menu has an associated pattern buffer, which is used to find the nearest match to the ASCII characters entered by the user. Whenever ASCII characters are given to menu_driver, it puts in to the pattern buffer. It also tries to find the nearest match to the pattern in the items list and moves current selection

to that item. The request `REQ_CLEAR_PATTERN` clears the pattern buffer. The request `REQ_BACK_PATTERN` deletes the previous character in the pattern buffer. In case the pattern matches more than one item then the matched items can be cycled through `REQ_NEXT_MATCH` and `REQ_PREV_MATCH` which move the current selection to the next and previous matches respectively.

Mouse Requests

In case of `KEY_MOUSE` requests, according to the mouse position an action is taken accordingly. The action to be taken is explained in the man page as, If the second argument is the `KEY_MOUSE` special key, the associated mouse event is translated into one of the above pre-defined requests. Currently only clicks in the user window (e.g. inside the menu display area or the decoration window) are handled. If you click above the display region of the menu, a `REQ_SCR_ULINE` is generated, if you doubleclick a `REQ_SCR_UPAGE` is generated and if you tripleclick a `REQ_FIRST_ITEM` is generated. If you click below the display region of the menu, a REQ_SCR_DLINE is generated, if you doubleclick a `REQ_SCR_DPAGE` is generated and if you tripleclick a `REQ_LAST_ITEM` is generated. If you click at an item inside the display area of the menu, the menu cursor is positioned to that item.

Each of the above requests will be explained in the following lines with several examples whenever appropriate.

4.14.3 Menu Windows

Every menu created is associated with a window and a subwindow. The menu window displays any title or border associated with the menu. The menu subwindow displays the menu items currently available for selection. But we didn't specify any window or sub window in the simple example. When a window is not specified, **stdscr** is taken as the main window, and then menu system calculates the subwindow size required for the display of items. Then items are displayed in the calculated sub window. So let's play with these windows and display a menu with a border and a title.

```
#!/usr/bin/guile
-s
!#

(use-modules (srfi srfi-1)
             (ncurses curses)
             (ncurses menu))

(define stdscr (initscr))
(start-color!)
(cbreak!)
(noecho!)
(keypad! stdscr #t)
(init-pair! 1 COLOR_RED COLOR_BLACK)

(let* (;; Labels for the menu items
       (names '("Choice 1" "Choice 2" "Choice 3" "Choice 4" "Exit"))
```

```
        (descriptions '("Description 1" "Description 2" "Description 3"
                        "Description 4" ""))

        ;; Create menu items for each label
        (my-items (map (lambda (name desc) (new-item name desc))
                       names
                       descriptions))
        ;; Create the menu
        (my-menu (new-menu my-items))

        ;; Make a windows to hold the menu
        (my-menu-win (newwin 10 40 4 4)))

(keypad! my-menu-win #t)

;; Set the main window and subwindow
(set-menu-win! my-menu my-menu-win)
(set-menu-sub! my-menu (derwin my-menu-win 6 38 3 1))

;; Set the menu mark string
(set-menu-mark! my-menu " * ")

;; Print a border around the main window, and a title
(box my-menu-win 0 0)

(attr-on! my-menu-win (color-pair 1))
(move my-menu-win 1 16)
(addstr my-menu-win "My Menu")
(attr-off! my-menu-win (color-pair 1))

(move my-menu-win 2 0)
(addch my-menu-win (acs-ltee))
(move my-menu-win 2 1)
(hline my-menu-win (acs-hline) 38)
(move my-menu-win 2 39)
(addch my-menu-win (acs-rtee))

(move stdscr (- (lines) 2) 0)
(addstr stdscr "F1 to exit")
(refresh stdscr)

;; Post the menu
(post-menu my-menu)
(refresh my-menu-win)

;; Draw the menu
(move stdscr (- (lines) 2) 0)
```

```
(addstr stdscr "F1 to Exit")

;; Process the up and down arrow keys.  Break the loop if F1 is
;; pressed.  Ignore other keys.
(let loop ((c (getch my-menu-win)))
  (cond

    ;; Move down the menu when down arrow is pressed and then loop.
    ((eqv? c KEY_DOWN)
     (begin
       (menu-driver my-menu REQ_DOWN_ITEM)
       (loop (getch my-menu-win))))

    ;; Move up the menu when the up arrow is pressed and then loop.
    ((eqv? c KEY_UP)
     (begin
       (menu-driver my-menu REQ_UP_ITEM)
       (loop (getch my-menu-win))))

    ;; When enter is pressed, return the selection and quit.
    ((or (eqv? c KEY_ENTER)
         (eqv? c #\cr)
         (eqv? c #\nl))
     (begin
       (unpost-menu my-menu)
       (move stdscr (- (lines) 4) 0)
       (addstr stdscr
               (format #f "You selected item #~a: ~a"
                       (item-index (current-item my-menu))
                       (item-name (current-item my-menu))))
       (refresh stdscr)
       (sleep 2)))

    ;; If F1 is pressed, quit.  Otherwise, loop.
    ((not (eqv? c (key-f 1)))
     (loop (getch stdscr)))))

(endwin))
```

This example creates a menu with a title, border, a fancy line separating title and the items. As you can see, in order to attach a window to a menu the function set-menu-win! has to be used. Then we attach the sub window also. This displays the items in the sub window. You can also set the mark string which gets displayed to the left of the selected item with set-menu-mark!.

4.14.4 Scrolling Menus

If the subwindow given for a window is not big enough to show all the items, then the menu will be scrollable. When you are on the last item in the present list, if you send `REQ_DOWN_ITEM`, it gets translated into `REQ_SCR_DLINE` and the menu scrolls by one item. You can manually give `REQ_SCR_` operations to do scrolling.

4.15 Forms Library

Well, if you have seen those forms on web pages that take input from users and do various kinds of things, you might be wondering how one would create such form in a text mode display. It's quite difficult to write those nifty forms in plain ncurses. The forms library tries to provide a basic framework to build and maintain forms with ease. It has lots of features that manage validation, dynamic expression of fields, and so on. Let's see it in full flow.

A form is a collection of fields. Each field can be either a label (static text) or a data-entry location. The forms library also provides functions to divide forms into multiple pages.

4.15.1 The Basics

Forms are created in much the same way as menus. First, the fields related to the form are created with `new-field`. You can set options for the fields, so that they can be displayed with some fancy attributes, validated before the field looses focus, etc. Then the fields are attached to the form. After this, the form can be posted to display and is ready to receive inputs. Along similar lines to `menu-driver`, the form is manipulated with `form-driver`. We can send requests to `form-driver` to move focus to a certain field, move the cursor to the end of the field, and so on. After the user enters the values in the fields and validation is done, the form can be unposted and the memory allocated can be freed.

The general flow of control of a form program looks like this

1. Initialize curses
2. Create fields using `new-field`. You can specify the height and width of the field, and its position on the form.
3. Create the forms with `new-form` by specifying the fields to be attached.
4. Post the form with `form-post` and refresh the screen.
5. Process the user requests with a loop and do necessary updates to the form with `form-driver`.
6. Unpost the menu with `form-unpost`
7. If desired, explicitly free the memory allocated to menu with `free-form`.
8. If desired, explicitly free the memory allocated to menu item with `free-field`.
9. End curses.

The forms library is similar to the menu library. The following examples will explore various aspects of form processing. Let's stat the journey with a simple example first.

4.15.2 A Form Example

To use form library functions, you have to include (`ncurses form`).

```
#!/usr/bin/guile
!#

(use-modules (srfi srfi-1)
             (ncurses curses)
             (ncurses form))

;; Initialize curses
(define stdscr (initscr))
(cbreak!)
(noecho!)
(keypad!  stdscr #t)

;; Initialize the fields
(define field (list
               (new-field 1 10 4 18 0 0)
               (new-field 1 10 6 18 0 0)))

;; Set field options
;; Print a line for the options
(set-field-back!  (first field) A_UNDERLINE)
;; Don't go to the next field when this field is filled up
(field-opts-off!  (first field) O_AUTOSKIP)
(set-field-back!  (second field) A_UNDERLINE)
(field-opts-off!  (second field) O_AUTOSKIP)

;; Create the new form and post it
(define my-form (new-form field))
(post-form my-form)
(refresh stdscr)

(addstr stdscr "Value 1:" #:y 4 #:x 10)
(addstr stdscr "Value 2:" #:y 6 #:x 10)
(refresh stdscr)

;; Loop through to get user requests
(let loop ((ch (getch stdscr)))
  (if (not (eqv?  ch (key-f 1)))
      (cond
        ((eqv?  ch KEY_DOWN)
         (begin
           ;; Go to the end of the next field
           (form-driver my-form REQ_NEXT_FIELD)
           (form-driver my-form REQ_END_LINE)
           (loop (getch stdscr))))
        ((eqv?  ch KEY_UP)
         (begin
```

```
                ;; Go to the end of the previous field
                (form-driver my-form REQ_PREV_FIELD)
                (form-driver my-form REQ_END_LINE)
                (loop (getch stdscr))))
            (else
             (begin
               ;; Print any normal character
               (form-driver my-form ch)
               (loop (getch stdscr)))))))

      ;; Unpost the form
      (unpost-form my-form)


      (endwin)
```

The above example is pretty straightforward. It creates two fields with `new-field`. The procedure `new-field` takes height, width startx, starty, the number of off-screen rows, and number of additional working buffers. The fifth argument number of off-screen rows specified how much of the field to be shown. If it is zero, the entire field is always displayed; otherwise, the form will be scrollable when the user accesses undisplayed part of the field. The forms library allocates one buffer per field to store the data which the user enters. Using the last parameter to `new-field` we can specify it to allocate some additional buffers. These can be used for any purpose you like.

After creating the fields, the background attribute of both of them is set to an underscore with `set-field-back!`. The AUTOSKIP option is turned off using `field-opts-off!`. If this option is turned of, focus will move to the next field in the form once the active field is filled up completely.

After attaching the fields to the form, it is posted. Here on, user inputs are processed in the loop, by making corresponding request to `form-driver`. The details of all the request to `form-driver` are explained later.

4.15.3 Making it useful

The previous example does create a form and allow one to move between the fields, but, it doesn't perform the useful function of allowing the program to fetch the contents of those fields. Also, the basic editing features like BS and DELETE are not connected.

To make it useful, it needs a couple of important changes. First, it passes more of the important editing commands like BS and DELETE to the form driver for processing. Second, it fetches the final content of the fields as one would normally do in a form application.

A more complete editing loop might look like this

```
      ;; Loop through to get user requests
      (let loop ((ch (getch win)))
        (if (not (eqv? ch (key-f 1)))
            (begin
              (cond
                ((eqv? ch KEY_DOWN)
                 (begin
```

```
            ;; Go to the end of the next field
            (form-driver my-form REQ_NEXT_FIELD)
            (form-driver my-form REQ_END_LINE)))
         ((eqv? ch KEY_UP)
          (begin
            ;; Go to the end of the previous field
            (form-driver my-form REQ_PREV_FIELD)
            (form-driver my-form REQ_END_LINE)))
         ((eqv? ch KEY_LEFT)
          (form-driver my-form REQ_PREV_CHAR))
         ((eqv? ch KEY_RIGHT)
          (form-driver my-form REQ_NEXT_CHAR))
         ((eqv? ch KEY_DC)
          (form-driver my-form REQ_DEL_CHAR))
         ((eqv? ch KEY_BACKSPACE)
          (form-driver my-form REQ_DEL_PREV))
         (else
          (form-driver my-form ch)))
        (loop (getch win)))))
```

And, gathering the contents of the form can be accomplished like this:

```
;; Move the cursor to ensure that the last characters typed by the
;; user get committed to the field buffer.
(form-driver my-form REQ_LAST_FIELD)
;; Unpost the form
(unpost-form my-form)

;; Store the contents of the field
(let ((result1 (field-buffer (first field) 0))
      (result2 (field-buffer (second field) 0)))
  (endwin)
  (display (string-append "You typed " result1 " and " result2))
  (newline))
```

4.15.4 Playing with fields

Each form field is associated with lots of attributes. They can be manipulated to get the required effect.

4.15.4.1 Fetching Size and Location of Field

The parameters we have given at the time of creation of a field can be retrieved with `field-info`.

```
(field-info field)
```

The procedure `field-info` takes a field and returns a list: height, width, top, left, offscreen, and number of buffers.

The location of the field can be moved to a different position with `move-field`, but, only if this field hasn't become part of a form. (This function is thus mostly useless.)

```
(move-field field top left)
```

The justification to be done for the field can be fixed using the function `set-field-just!`

```
(set-field-just! field justification)
```

The justification mode value is the either `NO_JUSTIFICATION`, `JUSTIFY_RIGHT`, `JUSTIFY_LEFT`, or `JUSTIFY_CENTER`.

The procedure `field-just` returns the justification mode.

4.15.5 Field Display Attributes

As you have seen, in the above example, display attributes for the fields can be set with `set-field-fore!` and `set-field-back!`. These functions set foreground and background attributes of the fields. You can also specify a pad character that will be filled in the unfilled portion of the field. The pad character is set with a call to `set-field-pad!`. Default pad value is space. The functions `field-fore` , `field-back`, and `field-pad` can be used to query the present foreground background attributes and pad character for the field.

Though the functions seem quite simple, using colors with `set-field-fore!` may be frustrating in the beginning. Let me first explain about foreground and background attributes of a field. The foreground attribute is associated with the character. That means a character in the field is printed with the attribute you have set with `set-field-fore!`. Background attribute is the attribute used to fill background of field, whether any character is there or not. So what about colors? Since colors are always defined in pairs, what is the right way to display colored fields? Here's an example clarifying color attributes.

```
#!/usr/bin/guile
!#

(use-modules (srfi srfi-1)
             (ncurses curses)
             (ncurses form))

;; Initialize curses
(define stdscr (initscr))
(start-color!)
(cbreak!)
(noecho!)
(keypad!  stdscr #t)

;; Initialize the color pairs
(init-pair!  1 COLOR_WHITE COLOR_BLUE)
(init-pair!  2 COLOR_WHITE COLOR_BLUE)

;; Initialize the fields
(define field (list
               (new-field 1 10 4 18 0 0)
               (new-field 1 10 6 18 0 0)))

;; Set field options
```

```
(set-field-fore!  (first field) (color-pair 1))
(set-field-back!  (first field) (color-pair 2))
(field-opts-off!  (first field) O_AUTOSKIP)

(set-field-back!  (second field) A_UNDERLINE)
(field-opts-off!  (second field) O_AUTOSKIP)

;; Create the new form and post it
(define my-form (new-form field))
(post-form my-form)
(refresh stdscr)

(addstr stdscr "Value 1:" #:y 4 #:x 10)
(addstr stdscr "Value 2:" #:y 6 #:x 10)
(refresh stdscr)

;; Loop through to get user requests
(let loop ((ch (getch stdscr)))
  (if (not (eqv? ch (key-f 1)))
      (cond
        ((eqv? ch KEY_DOWN)
         (begin
           ;; Go to the end of the next field
           (form-driver my-form REQ_NEXT_FIELD)
           (form-driver my-form REQ_END_LINE)
           (loop (getch stdscr))))
        ((eqv? ch KEY_UP)
         (begin
           ;; Go to the end of the previous field
           (form-driver my-form REQ_PREV_FIELD)
           (form-driver my-form REQ_END_LINE)
           (loop (getch stdscr))))
        (else
         (begin
           ;; Print any normal character
           (form-driver my-form ch)
           (loop (getch stdscr)))))))

;; Unpost the form
(unpost-form my-form)

(endwin)
```

Play with the color pairs and try to understand the foreground and background attributes. Color pair 1 is used for the character that have been typed into the form, and color pair 2 is used for the empty spaces in the form.

4.15.6 Field Option Bits

There is also a large collection of field option bits you can set to control various aspects of forms processing. You can manipulate them with the procedures `set-field-opts!`, `field-opts-on!`, `field-opts-off!`, and `field-opts`.

The function `set-field-opts!` can be used to directly set attributes of a field or you can chose to switch a few attributes on and off with `field-opts-on!` and `field-opts-off!`. You can query the attributes of a field with `field-opts`. The following is a list of available options. By default, all options are on.

O_VISIBLE

Controls whether the field is visible on the screen. Can be used during form processing to hide or pop up fields depending on the value of parent fields.

O_ACTIVE

Controls whether the field is active during forms processing (i.e. visited by form navigation keys). Can be used to make labels or derived fields with buffer values alterable by the forms application, not the user.

O_PUBLIC

Controls whether data is displayed during field entry. If this option is turned off on a field, the library will accept and edit data in that field, but it will not be displayed and the visible field cursor will not move. You can turn off the O_PUBLIC bit to define password fields.

O_EDIT

Controls whether the field's data can be modified. When this option is off, all editing requests except REQ_PREV_CHOICE and REQ_NEXT_CHOICE will fail. Such read-only fields may be useful for help messages.

O_WRAP

Controls word-wrapping in multiline fields. Normally, when any character of a (blank-separated) word reaches the end of the current line, the entire word is wrapped to the next line (assuming there is one). When this option is off, the word will be split across the line break.

O_BLANK

Controls field blanking. When this option is on, entering a character at the first field position erases the entire field (except for the just-entered character).

O_AUTOSKIP

Controls automatic skip to next field when this one fills. Normally, when the forms user tries to type more data into a field than will fit, the editing location jumps to the next field. When this option is off, the user's cursor will hang at the end of the field. This option is ignored in dynamic fields that have not reached their size limit.

O_NULLOK

Controls whether validation is applied to blank fields. Normally, it is not; the user can leave a field blank without invoking the usual validation check on exit. If this option is off on a field, exit from it will invoke a validation check.

O_PASSOK

> Controls whether validation occurs on every exit, or only after the field is modified. Normally the latter is true. Setting O_PASSOK may be useful if your field's validation function may change during forms processing.

O_STATIC

> Controls whether the field is fixed to its initial dimensions. If you turn this off, the field becomes dynamic and will stretch to fit entered data.

A field's options cannot be changed while the field is currently selected. However, options may be changed on posted fields that are not current.

The option values are bit-masks and can be composed with logior in the obvious way. You have seen the usage of watching off O_AUTOSKIP option. The following example clarified usage of some more options. One field is a constant, uneditable field, that you cannot move to by using the arrow keys. The other field is a password-like field where the characters are hidden from view.

```
#!/usr/local/bin/guile
!#

(use-modules (srfi srfi-1)
             (ncurses curses)
             (ncurses form))

;; Constants
(define STARTX 15)
(define STARTY 4)
(define WIDTH 25)
(define N_FIELDS 2)

;; Initialize curses
(define stdscr (initscr))
(cbreak!)
(noecho!)
(keypad! stdscr #t)

;; Initialize the fields
(define field (map-in-order
               (lambda (y)
                 (new-field 1
                            WIDTH
                            (+ (* y 2) STARTY)
                            STARTX
                            0
                            0))
               (iota N_FIELDS)))

;; Set field options
```

```
(set-field-back! (first field) A_UNDERLINE)
;; Don't go to the next field when this field is filled up

;; This field is a static label
(field-opts-off! (first field) O_ACTIVE)

;; This field is like a password field
(field-opts-off! (second field) O_PUBLIC)
(field-opts-off! (second field) O_AUTOSKIP)

;; Create the new form and post it
(define my-form (new-form field))
(post-form my-form)
(refresh)

(set-field-just! (first field) JUSTIFY_CENTER)
(set-field-buffer! (first field) 0 "This is a static field")

(addstr "Field 1:" #:y STARTY #:x (- STARTX 10))
(addstr "Field 2:" #:y (+ STARTY 2) #:x (- STARTX 10))
(refresh)

;; Loop through to get user requests
(let loop ((ch (getch)))
  (if (not (eqv? ch (key-f 1)))
      (cond
        ((eqv? ch KEY_DOWN)
         (begin
           ;; Go to the end of the next field
           (form-driver my-form REQ_NEXT_FIELD)
           (form-driver my-form REQ_END_LINE)
           (loop (getch))))
        ((eqv? ch KEY_UP)
         (begin
           ;; Go to the end of the previous field
           (form-driver my-form REQ_PREV_FIELD)
           (form-driver my-form REQ_END_LINE)
           (loop (getch))))
        (else
         (begin
           ;; Print any normal character
           (form-driver my-form ch)
           (loop (getch))))))))

;; Unpost the form
(unpost-form my-form)
```

```
(endwin)
```

4.15.7 Field Status

The field status specifies whether the field has been edited. It is initially #f and when the user enters something and the data buffer gets modified, it becomes #t. So a field's status can be queried to find out if it has been modified or not.

The two procedures that work with field status are set-field-status! and field-status?. The procedure field-status? returns the current state, and set-field-status! can be used to set the state.

4.15.8 Variable-Sized Fields

If you want a dynamically changing field with variable width, this is the feature you want to put to full use. This will allow the user to enter more data than the original size of the field and let the field grow. According to the field orientation it will scroll horizontally or vertically to incorporate the new data.

To make a field dynamically growable, the option O_STATIC should be turned off. This can be done with

```
(field-opts-off! field O_STATIC)
```

It is usually not advisable to allow a field to grow infinitely.. You can set a maximum limit to the growth of the field with set-max-field.

The field info for a dynamically growable field can be retrieved with the procedure dynamic-field-info.

Recall the library routine new-field; a new field created with height set to one will be defined to a one line field. A new field created with height greater than one will be defined to be a multi-line field.

A one line field with O_STATIC turned off (dynamically growable) will contain a single fixed row, but, the number of columns can increase if the user enters more data than the initial field will hole. The number of columns displayed will remain fixed and the additional data will scroll horizontally.

A multiline field with O_STATIC turned off (dynamically growable) will contain a fixed number of columns, but, the number of rows can increase if the user enters more data than the initial field will hold. The number of rows displayed will remain fixed and the additional data will scroll vertically.

4.15.9 Form Windows

The form windows concept is pretty much similar to menu windows. Every form is associated with a main window and a subwindow. The form main window displays any title or border associated or whatever the user wishes. The subwindow contains all the fields and displays them according to their position. This gives the flexibility of manipulating fancy form displays easily.

Since this pretty similar to menu windows, I am providing a very similar example.

```
#!/usr/local/bin/guile
!#
```

```
(use-modules (srfi srfi-1)
             (ncurses curses)
             (ncurses form))

;; Helper procedure to center a text
(define (print-in-middle win starty startx width str color)
  (let ((length (string-length str)))

    (attr-on! win color)
    (addstr win str
            #:y starty
            #:x (+ startx (/ (- width length) 2)))

    (attr-off! win color)
    (refresh)))


;; Initialize curses
(define stdscr (initscr))
(start-color!)
(cbreak!)
(noecho!)
(keypad! stdscr #t)

;;Initialize a few color pairs
(init-pair! 1 COLOR_RED COLOR_BLACK)

(define field (list
               (new-field 1 10 6 1 0 0)
               (new-field 1 10 8 1 0 0)))

;; Set field options
(set-field-back! (first field) A_UNDERLINE)
(field-opts-off! (first field) O_AUTOSKIP)

(set-field-back! (second field) A_UNDERLINE)
(field-opts-off! (second field) O_AUTOSKIP)

;; Create a new form
(define my-form (new-form field))

;; Calculate the area associated with the form
(define xy (scale-form my-form))
(define rows (car xy))
(define cols (cadr xy))
```

```scheme
;; Create the window to be associated with the form
(define my-form-win (newwin (+ 4 rows)
                            (+ 4 cols)
                            4
                            4))
(keypad! my-form-win #t)

;; Set main window and subwindow
(set-form-win! my-form my-form-win)
(set-form-sub! my-form (derwin my-form-win rows cols 2 2))

;; Print a border around the main window and print a title
(box my-form-win 0 0)
(print-in-middle my-form-win 1 0 (+ cols 4) "My Form" (color-pair 1))

(post-form my-form)
(refresh my-form-win)

(addstr stdscr "Use UP, DOWN arrow keys to switch between fields"
        #:y (- (lines) 2) #:x 0)
(refresh stdscr)

;; Loop through to get user requests
(let loop ((ch (getch my-form-win)))
  (if (not (eqv? ch (key-f 1)))
      (cond
        ((eqv? ch KEY_DOWN)
         (begin
           ;; Go to the end of the next field
           (form-driver my-form REQ_NEXT_FIELD)
           (form-driver my-form REQ_END_LINE)
           (loop (getch my-form-win))))
        ((eqv? ch KEY_UP)
         (begin
           ;; Go to the end of the previous field
           (form-driver my-form REQ_PREV_FIELD)
           (form-driver my-form REQ_END_LINE)
           (loop (getch my-form-win))))
        (else
         (begin
           ;; Print any normal character
           (form-driver my-form ch)
           (loop (getch my-form-win))))))))

;; Unpost the form
(unpost-form my-form)
```

`(endwin)`

4.15.10 Field Validation

By default, a field will accept any data input by the user. It is possible to attach validation to the field. Then any attempt by the user to leave the field while it contains data that doesn't match the validation type will fail.. Some validation types also have a character-validity check for each type a character is entered in the field.

Validation can be attached by using the `set-field-type!` procedure and queried with the `field-type` procedure.

The form driver validates the data in a field only when data is entered by the end-user. Validation does not occur when the application program changes the field value with `set-field-buffer!`.

The validation types are as follows.

TYPE_ALPHA

> This field type accepts alphabetic data; no blanks, no digits, no special characters. It takes a width argument that sets a minimum width of the data. The user has to enter at least that number of characters be fore he can leave the field. Typically you'll want to set this to the field width. If it's greater than the field width, the validation check will always fail. A minimum width of zero makes field completion optional.

> `(set-field-type! field TYPE_ALPHA width)`

TYPE_ALNUM

> This field type accepts alphabetic data and digits. No blanks, no special characters. It also has a width argument.

> `(set-field-type! field TYPE_ALPHA width)`

TYPE_ENUM

> This type allows you to restrict a field's values to be among a specified set of string values (for example, the two-letter postal codes for US states). It takes as input a list of strings. It can be set up as either case sensitive or case insensitive. When the user exits, the validation procedure tries to complete the data in the buffer to a valid entry. If a complete choice string has been entered, it is, of course, valid. But it is also possible to enter a prefix of a valid string and have it completed for you.

> By default, if you enter such a prefix and it matches more than on value in the string list, the prefix will be completed to the first matching value. If the check-unique option is chosen, the prefix match must be unique to be valid.

> `(set-field-type! field TYPE_ENUM valuelist checkcase checkunique)`

TYPE_INTEGER

> Valid characters consist of an optional leading minus and digits. A range check is performed on exit. If the range maximum is less than or equal to the minimum, the range is ignored.

> `(set-field-type! field TYPE_INTEGER zero-padding min max)`

> If the value passes its range check, it is padded with as many leading zero digits as necessary to meet the padding requirement.

```
TYPE_NUMERIC
```
        This accepts a decimal number.

            `(set-field-type! field TYPE_NUMERIC digits-of-precision min max)`

        Valid characters consist of a leading minus and digits, possibly including a decimate point. The range check is performed on exit.

        If the value passes its range check, it is padded with as many trailing zero digits as necessary to meet the padding argument.

```
TYPE_REGEXP
```
        This field type accepts a regular expression, and thus can be used to perform other types of range checks.

4.15.11 The Form Driver: The Work Horse of the System

The `form-driver` procedure plays a very important role in the forms system. All types of requests to forms should be funneled through `form-driver`.

As you have seen some of the examples above, you have to be in a loop looking for user input and then decide whether it is a field data or a form request. The form requests are then passes to `form-driver` to do the work.

The requests roughly can be divided into the following categories. Different request and their usage is explained below.

4.15.11.1 Page Navigation Requests

These requests cause page-level moves through the form, triggering display of a new form screen. A form can be made of multiple pages. If you have a big form with lots of fields and logical sections, then you can divide the form into pages. The function `set-new-page` sets a new page at the field specified.

Also, the following requests, when passed to the form driver, all you to move to different pages.

- REQ_NEXT_PAGE Move to the next form page.
- REQ_PREV_PAGE Move to the previous form page.
- REQ_FIRST_PAGE Move to the first form page.
- REQ_LAST_PAGE Move to the last form page.

These are cyclic. The moving to the next page after the last page put you at the top.

4.15.11.2 Inter-Field Navigation Requests

- REQ_NEXT_FIELD Move to the next field
- REQ_PREV_FIELD Move to the previous field
- REQ_FIRST_FIELD Move to the first field.
- REQ_LAST_FIELD Move to the last field.
- REQ_SNEXT_FIELD Move to the sorted next field.
- REQ_SPREV_FIELD Move to the sorted previous field.
- REQ_SFIRST_FIELD Move to sorted first field.
- REQ_SLAST_FIELD Move to sorted last field.

- REQ_LEFT_FIELD Move left to field.
- REQ_RIGHT_FIELD Move right to field.
- REQ_UP_FIELD Move up one field.
- REQ_DOWN_FIELD Move down one field.

These requests treat fields as cyclic, moving off the end of the page will return you to the top.

5 Curses Reference

The guile-ncurses package provides the following modules:

1. (ncurses curses): Basic functionality and input/output.
2. (ncurses panel): A library for managing overlapping windows.
3. (ncurses menu): A library for menu creation.
4. (ncurses form): A library for creating text-based form screens.
5. (ncurses slk): The soft keys functions.

5.1 The naming of routines

When you look at this library, it may seem that exclamation points and question marks were sprinkled at random on the ends of curses functions. There is actually a thought process behind it: it isn't just chaos.

- A procedure that returns #t or #f and *does not* change the behavior of the system in any way ends in a question mark, e.g. has-ic?.
- But, a procedure that returns #t or #f and *does* change the behavior of the system does not end in a question mark, e.g. beep.
- A procedure that changes any property of curses but does not write to a window or screen ends in an exclamation point, e.g. bkgdset!.
- Any procedure that writes to a window or screen does not in an exclamation point, e.g. addch.
- Curses integer constants are capitalized and use underscores, for example A_BOLD.
- Curses procedures are not capitalized, even if they were capitalized macros in the C Ncurses library, for example lines and tabsize.

5.2 The basic curses library: (ncurses curses)

These are the functions in the (ncurses curses) module.

The procedures in the curses library closely follow the functions in the C-language API. Most of the procedures in the library have approximately the same name and arguments as the functions in the C-language API.

5.2.1 Overview

The GNU Guile-Ncurses library routines give the user a terminal-independent method of updating character screens with reasonable optimization.

The package supports overall screen, window and pad manipulation; output to windows and pads; reading terminal input; control over terminal and curses input and output options; environment query routines; color manipulation; use of soft label keys; terminfo capabilities; and access to low-level terminal-manipulation routines.

To initialize the routines, the routine initscr or newterm must be called before any of the other routines that deal with windows and screens are used. The routine endwin must be called before exiting. To get character-at-a-time input without echoing (most interactive, screen oriented programs want this), the following sequence should be used:

```
(cbreak!)
(noecho!)
```

Most programs would additionally use the sequence:

```
(nonl!)
(intrflush! #f)
(keypad! stdscr #t))
```

Before a curses program is run, the tab stops of the terminal should be set and its initialization strings, if defined, must be output. This can be done by executing the **tput** init command after the shell environment variable **TERM** has been exported. **tset** is usually responsible for doing this. [See terminfo for further details.]

The Guile-Ncurses library permits manipulation of data structures, the **#<window>** type, which can be thought of as two-dimensional arrays of characters representing all or part of a CRT screen. A default window, conventionally called **stdscr**, which is the size of the terminal screen, is supplied. The **#<window>** information for stdscr is returned by calling the procedure **initscr**. Other windows may be created with **newwin**.

Note that **(ncurses curses)** does not easily handle overlapping windows. Overlapping windows usually require the use of the **(ncurses panel)** library. Without the panel library, you can either position everything on screen by hand or divide the screen into tiled windows. Chose one of the two strategies and stick with it. Mixing the two will result in unpredictable, and undesired, effects.

Windows are referred to by variables declared as **#<window>**. These data structures are manipulated with routines described here. Among those, the most basic routines are **move** and **addch**. **move** places the cursor at a location in a buffer, and **addch** puts a character at that location.

After using routines to manipulate a window, **refresh** is called, telling curses to make the user's CRT screen look like array of characters in a **#<window>** buffer. Other information about the character may also be stored with each character.

Special windows called *pads* may also be manipulated. These are windows which are not constrained to the size of the screen and whose contents need not be completely displayed.

In addition to drawing characters on the screen, video attributes and colors may be supported, causing the characters to show up in such modes as underlined, in reverse video, or in color on terminals that support such display enhancements. Line drawing characters may be specified to be output. On input, curses is also able to translate arrow and function keys that transmit escape sequences into single values. The video attributes, line drawing characters, and input values use names, such as **A_REVERSE**, **(acs-hline)**, and **KEY_LEFT**.

If the environment variables **LINES** and **COLUMNS** are set, or if the program is executing in a window environment, line and column information in the environment will override information read by terminfo.

If the environment variable **TERMINFO** is defined, any program using curses checks for a local terminal definition before checking in the standard places. For example, if **TERM** is set to **xterm**, then the compiled terminal definition is found in **/usr/share/terminfo/x/xterm**

(The "x" is copied from the first letter of "xterm" to avoid creation of huge directories.) However, if **TERMINFO** is set to **$HOME/myterms**, curses first checks **$HOME/myterms/x/xterm**, and if that fails, it then checks the standard location.

This is useful for developing experimental definitions or when write permission in /usr/share/terminfo is not available.

The getter procedures (lines) and (cols) are defined in (ncurses curses) and will be return the size of the screen at the time initscr was called.

5.2.1.1 The Coordinate System

The move routine and routines that take #:y and #:x arguments use a screen based coordinate system. The coordinate y always refers to the row (of the window), and x always refers to the column. The upper left-hand corner is always (0,0). y increases as one moves down the window, and x increases as one moves left.

5.2.2 Features determined at compile time

When the Guile-Ncurses library was compiled, tests were run to see which features could be enabled. There are two variables that describe the capabilities of this build of Guile-Ncurses.

%wide-ncurses   [Constant]
> This is set to #t if Guile-Ncurses is using the features of the wide ncurses library libncursesw. Otherwise, it is #f.

%ucs4-chars   [Constant]
> This is set to #t if Guile-Ncurses expects that characters are stored as UCS4 codepoints, such as in Guile 2.0.x. It is #f if Guile-Ncurses expects that characters are 8-bit only and stored according to the current 8-bit locale.

5.2.3 Curses screen initialization and manipulation routines

initscr is normally the first curses routine to call when initializing a program. A few special routines sometimes need to be called before it; these are slk-init, %filter, ripoffline, use-env. For multiple-terminal applications, newterm may be called before initscr.

initscr   [Procedure]
> The initscr code determines the terminal type and initializes all curses data structures. initscr also causes the first call to refresh to clear the screen.
>
> The #<window> returned by initscr should be held in a variable that exists for the lifetime of a curses program. If it is garbage collected, the window will become unusable.
>
> If errors occur, initscr throws and error and exits; otherwise, a #<window> referencing stdscr is returned.

cols   [Procedure]
lines   [Procedure]
> These procedures, if called after initscr has been called, will return the size of the screen at the time initscr was called.

newterm *type outport inport*   [Procedure]
> The procedure newterm initializes curses for a given terminal type *type* on specific curses port *inport* and *outport*. The newterm function relies on some relatively obscure GNU C library functions and thus may not be available on non-GNU systems.

The routine **newterm** should be called once for each terminal. It returns a variable of type **#<screen>** which should be saved as a reference to that terminal. *type* is the type of the terminal to be used in place of **$TERM**. *outport* is a port that will receive the output to the terminal.

IMPORTANT: These ports must be file ports. The underlying ncurses library extracts the file descriptor from the port and uses that to write to the screen. Also, these ports will be closed by **newterm** and cannot be reused.

newterm will internally use a duplicate port to the file pointed to by *inport*. *inport* won't be used except to get a file descriptor for the underlying file.

Immediately following the call to newterm, one should create a window for the terminal by using the **stdscr** procedure. So the standard way to initialize it would be something like.

```
(newterm "vt220" outport inport)
(define stdscr (stdscr))
```

This routine will throw an error if the terminal could not be created.

A program that outputs to more than one terminal should use the **newterm** routine for each terminal instead of **initscr**. A program that needs to inspect capabilities, so it can continue to run in a line-oriented mode if the terminal cannot support a screen-oriented program, would also use **newterm**. The program must also call **endwin** for each terminal being used before exiting from curses. If **newterm** is called more than once for the same terminal, the first terminal referred to must be the last one for which **endwin** is called.

endwin   [Procedure]
   A program should always call **endwin** before exiting or escaping from curses mode temporarily. This routine restores TTY modes, moves the cursor to the lower left-hand corner of the screen and resets the terminal into the proper non-visual mode. Calling **refresh** or **doupdate** after a temporary escape causes the program to resume visual mode.

   Its return value is **#t** if the terminal can be restored to its behavior (as in **reset-shell-mode**), or **#f** otherwise. If the terminal was created by **newterm**, then this will usually return **#f** since input file had no previous mode.

isendwin?   [Procedure]
   The **isendwin?** routine returns **#t** if **endwin** has been called without any subsequent calls to **refresh**, and **#f** otherwise.

set-term *new*   [Procedure]
   The **set-term** routine is used to switch between different terminals. If the program has created multiple terminal using the **newterm** procedure, then **set-term** can be called to set one of those terminal to be the current terminal on which all the curses procedures will operate. The screen reference *new* becomes the new current terminal. This is the only routine which manipulates **#<screen>** types; all other routines affect only the current terminal.

   The return value is unspecified.

delscreen *screen*   [Procedure]

> The delscreen routine frees storage associated with the *screen* data structure. The **endwin** routine does not do this, so **delscreen** should be called after **endwin** if a particular *screen* is no longer needed. Trying to use a screen after it has been freed will likely result in "bad state" errors.
>
> The return value is unspecified.

5.2.4 Errors and Exceptions

The curses library uses SRFI-34's raise and SRFI-35 conditions to signal errors.

> All errors in the curses library are of type **&curses-error**.

curses-error? *err*   [Procedure]

> Returns true if *err* is a **&curses-error**

The wrong type error has two fields: **arg** and **expected-type**.

curses-wrong-type-arg-error? *err*   [Procedure]
curses-wrong-type-arg-error:arg *err*   [Procedure]
curses-wrong-type-arg-error:expected-type *err*   [Procedure]

> The predicate and accessors for the wrong type error.

5.2.5 Making rendered characters

Many curses functions take rendered, complex characters: characters with associated color and attribute information.

For those who are familiar with the C API for ncurses, you know that a rendered character is either a **chtype**, which is a 32-bit integer containing an 8-bit **char** and 24-bits of color and rendering information, or is a **cchar_t**, which is one or more **wchar_t** characters plus associated color and rendering information. Guile-Ncurses abstracts away the difference between these two types and presents a consistent API for both. The Guile-Ncurses complex rendered character will get converted automatically to **chtype** or **cchar_t** when necessary.

There is a family of functions to convert unrendered, simple characters or strings to rendered complex characters and strings.

blink *x*   [Procedure]
bold *x*   [Procedure]
dim *x*   [Procedure]
horizontal *x*   [Procedure]
invis *x*   [Procedure]
left *x*   [Procedure]
low *x*   [Procedure]
normal *x*   [Procedure]
protect *x*   [Procedure]
inverse *x*   [Procedure]
right *x*   [Procedure]
standout *x*   [Procedure]
top *x*   [Procedure]

underline _x_   [Procedure]
vertical _x_   [Procedure]

    These procedures take _x_, which can be either a simple character, a complex character, a simple string, or a complex string, and returns a rendered character or string with the attribute blink, bold, dim, horizontal, invisible, left, low, normal, protect, inverse, right, top, underline, or vertical, respectively. If the input _x_ was a rendered character or a rendered string, the old attributes are replaced. If _x_ was a rendered character or string with an associated color pair, the returned character or string will have the same associated color pair.

    Note that whether these attributes can actually be visualized depends on the capabilities of the terminal itself. Most terminals can handle bold, dim, inverse, and sometimes blink, underline and invisible. The rest should probably not be used.

blink-on _x_   [Procedure]
bold-on _x_   [Procedure]
dim-on _x_   [Procedure]
horizontal-on _x_   [Procedure]
invis-on _x_   [Procedure]
left-on _x_   [Procedure]
low-on _x_   [Procedure]
normal-on _x_   [Procedure]
protect-on _x_   [Procedure]
inverse-on _x_   [Procedure]
right-on _x_   [Procedure]
standout-on _x_   [Procedure]
top-on _x_   [Procedure]
underline-on _x_   [Procedure]
vertical-on _x_   [Procedure]

    These procedures take _x_, which can be either a simple character, a complex character, a simple string, or a complex string. If _x_ is a simple character or simple string, it sets its rendering to blink, bold, dim, horizontal, invisible, left, low, normal, protect, inverse, right, top, underline, or vertical, respectively. If the input _x_ was a rendered character or a rendered string, these attributes are added to the rendered character.

    Most terminals can't actually visualize multiple attributes on a single character: some terminals can handle the combination of blink and bold, bold and underline, or inverse and bold.

blink-off _x_   [Procedure]
bold-off _x_   [Procedure]
dim-off _x_   [Procedure]
horizontal-off _x_   [Procedure]
invis-off _x_   [Procedure]
left-off _x_   [Procedure]
low-off _x_   [Procedure]
normal-off _x_   [Procedure]
protect-off _x_   [Procedure]
inverse-off _x_   [Procedure]

right-off *x*   [Procedure]
standout-off *x*   [Procedure]
top-off *x*   [Procedure]
underline-off   [Procedure]
vertical-off *x*   [Procedure]
> These procedures take *x*, which can be either a simple character, a complex character, a simple string, or a complex string. If *x* is a simple character or simple string, it sets its rendering to normal. If the input *x* was a rendered character or a rendered string and had the given attribute, these attributes is removed from the resulting rendered character.

color *n x*   [Procedure]
> These procedure takes *x*, which can be either a simple character, a complex character, a simple string, or a complex string. It returns a rendered character or string with an associated color pair *n*.
>
> This procedure should only be used if **start-color** has been called.

There are a set of primitives to operate directly on complex characters.

xchar? *c*   [Procedure]
> Returns **#t** if *c* is a complex character.

xchar-attr *c*   [Procedure]
xchar-color *c*   [Procedure]
xchar-chars *c*   [Procedure]
> These three procedures return the attributes, color pair number, and list of constiuent characters of a complex character, respectively.

set-xchar-attr! *c attr*   [Procedure]
set-xchar-color! *c color-pair-number*   [Procedure]
set-xchar-chars! *c list-of-chars*   [Procedure]
> These procedures directly set the attributes, color-pair number, and the list of characters of a complex character, respectively.

Complex characters can have a base character and a set of accent characters that overwrite the base character. That is why **set-xchar-chars!** takes a list of characters, instead of a single character. But, for these complex characters to be rendered correctly on the terminal, you need both a terminal that can do overstrike characters and you need to have compiled with the wide Ncurses library. If either of these conditions are not true, only the first character in the list of characters will appear on the screen.

There are also a couple of low-level functions to do conversion between C characters and Guile characters.

%scheme-char-from-c-char *c*   [Procedure]
> Given an 8-bit integer *c* that represents a C character in the current locale, this returns the associated scheme character.

%scheme-char-to-c-char *c*   [Procedure]
> This returns an 8-bit integer that is the C representation of character **c** in the current locale. If the character cannot be represented in the current locale, it will return the integer 63, which is the ASCII code for the question mark.

%scheme-char-from-c-wchar *c*   [Procedure]

> Given an integer *c* that represents a wchar_t representation of a C wide character, this returns the associated scheme character.

%scheme-char-to-c-wchar *c*   [Procedure]

> This returns an integer that is the C `wchar_t` representation of character *c*. If the character cannot be represented in the current locale, it will return the integer #xFFFD, which is the Unicode codepoint for the replacement character.

5.2.6 Outputting characters

There are two primary functions that add a rendered character to a curses window, and then advance the cursor.

addch *win ch #:key y x*   [Procedure]

> The `addch` routine puts the rendered character *ch* into the given window at its current window position, which is then advanced. If the advance is at the right margin, the cursor automatically wraps to the beginning of the next line. At the bottom of the current scrolling region, if `scrollok!` is enabled, the scrolling region is scrolled up one line.
>
> If *ch* is a tab, newline, or backspace, the cursor is moved appropriately within the window. Backspace moves the cursor one character left; at the left edge of a window it does nothing. Newline does a `clrtoeol`, then moves the cursor to the window left margin on the next line, scrolling the window if on the last line. Tabs are considered to be at every eighth column. The tab interval may be altered with the `set-tabsize!` procedure.
>
> If *ch* is any control character other than `TAB`, `CR`, or `BS`, it is drawn in ^X notation. Calling `inch` after adding a control character does not return the character itself, but instead returns the ^-representation of the control character.
>
> Since *ch* is a rendered character, the rendition will be applied to the character when it is put on the screen.
>
> This function returns `#t` on success and `#f` otherwise. A `#f` usually indicates an attempt to add a character that won't fit on the screen or that would cause a wrap or scroll in a window that doesn't wrap or scroll.

echochar *win ch #:key y x*   [Procedure]

> The `echochar` routine is equivalent to a call to `addch` followed by a call to `refresh`. The knowledge that only a single character is being output allows for efficiency.
>
> This function returns `#t` on success and `#f` otherwise. A `#f` usually indicates an attempt to add a character that won't fit on the screen or that would cause a wrap or scroll in a window that doesn't wrap or scroll.

tabsize   [Procedure]

> Returns the current tabsize for this screen. The default is eight.

set-tabsize! *tab*   [Procedure]

> Sets the tabsize for this screen to *tab* characters.
>
> Its return value is unspecified.

5.2.6.1 Line Graphics

The line-graphics procedures may be used to add line drawing characters to the screen with routines of the addch family. Not all terminals have line-graphics characters. There is a default character listed below is used if the acsc capability doesn't define a terminal-specific replacement for it. The names are taken from VT100 nomenclature. Each of these procedures takes no arguments and returns a rendered character with the 'normal' attribute and with the default color pair. The following prints a less-than-or-equal-to sign to the window win, for example.

```
(addch win (normal (acs-lequal)))
```

The set of line-graphics characters is given in Table 5.1.

name	default	description
acs-block	#	solid square block
acs-board	#	board of squares
acs-btee	+	bottom tee
acs-bullet	o	bullet
acs-ckboard	:	checker board (stipple)
acs-darrow	v	arrow pointing down
acs-degree	'	degree symbol
acs-diamond	+	diamond
acs-gequal	>	greater-than-or-equal-to
acs-hline	-	horizontal line
acs-lantern	#	lantern symbol
acs-larrow	<	arrow pointing left
acs-lequal	<	less-than-or-equal-to
acs-llcorner	+	lower left-hand corner
acs-lrcorner	+	lower right-hand corner
acs-ltee	+	left tee
acs-nequal	!	not-equal
acs-pi	*	greek pi
acs-plminus	#	plus/minus
acs-plus	+	plus
acs-rarrow	>	arrow pointing right
acs-rtee	+	right tee
acs-s1	-	scan line 1
acs-s3	-	scan line 3
acs-s7	-	scan line 7
acs-s9	_	scan line 9
acs-sterling	f	pound-sterling symbol
acs-ttee	+	top tee
acs-uarrow	^	arrow pointing up
acs-ulcorner	+	upper left-hand corner
acs-urcorner	+	upper right-hand corner
acs-vline	|	vertical line

Table 5.1: the line-graphics procedures

5.2.7 Outputting strings

addstr *win #:key y x n*   [Procedure]
This routine writes the characters of the unrendered simple string *str* on the given window. When called with *n* it writes at most n characters. If *n* is -1, then the entire string will be added, up to the maximum number of characters that will fit on the line, or until a terminating null is reached.

It returns `#f` upon failure and `#t` on success. Failure usually indicates at attempt to write beyond the borders of the window or to write in a place that would cause scroll or wrap on a window that doesn't support it.

`addchstr` *win chstr #:key y x n*   [Procedure]

These routines copy the rendered, complex string *chstr* into the window image structure at and after the current cursor position. If *n* is defined, copy at most *n* elements, but no more than will fit on the line. If *n* equals -1 or if it is undefined, then the whole string is copied, to the maximum number of characters that will fit on the line.

The window cursor is not advanced, and these routines work faster than `addstr`. On the other hand, they do not perform any kind of checking (such as for the newline, backspace, or carriage return characters), they do not advance the current cursor position, they do not expand other control characters to ^-escapes, and they truncate the string if it crosses the right margin, rather than wrapping it around to the newline.

It returns `#f` upon failure and `#t` on success.

5.2.8 Character and window attribute control routines

These routines manipulate the current attributes of the named window. The current attributes of a window apply to all characters that are written into the window with `addch` and `addstr`. Attributes are a property of the character, and move with the character through any scrolling and insert/delete line/character operations. To the extent possible, they are displayed as appropriate modifications to the graphic rendition of characters put on the screen.

`attr-set!` *win attrs #:optional color*   [Procedure]
`attr-on!` *win attrs*   [Procedure]
`attr-off!` *win attrs*   [Procedure]
`standend!` *win*   [Procedure]
`standout!` *win*   [Procedure]

The routine `attr-set!` sets the current rendition (attributes and color pair) of the given window to *attrs*. Optionally, you may split the color-pair information as a third parameter.

attrs is one of the attribute constants: there is an attribute constant for each of the attributes mentioned in Section 5.2.5 [Making rendered characters], page 59: A_BLINK, A_BOLD, A_DIM, A_INVIS, A_NORMAL, A_PROTECT, A_REVERSE, A_STANDOUT, A_UNDERLINE, A_HORIZONTAL, A_LEFT, A_LOW, A_RIGHT, A_TOP, A_VERTICAL.

The following two calls are equivalent:

```
(attr-set! win (logior A_BOLD (color-pair 1)))
```

or

```
(attr-set! win A_BOLD 1)
```

The routine `attr-off!` turns off the named attributes without turning any other attributes on or off. The routine `attr-on!` turns on the named attributes without affecting any others. The routine `standout!` is the same as (`attr-on!` A_STANDOUT). The routine `standend!` is the same as (`attr-set!` A_NORMAL) or (`attr-set!` 0), that is, it turns off all attributes.

The return value of these routines are undefined. They can throw an exception if curses is in a bad state.

The `attr-set!` and related routines do not affect the attributes used when erasing portions of the window. For functions which modify the attributes used for erasing and clearing See Section 5.2.10 [Window background manipulation routines], page 67.

`color-set!` *win color-pair-number*   [Procedure]
> The routine `color-set!` sets the current color of the given window to the foreground/background combination described by the *color-pair-number*.
>
> The return value is unspecified, but, it can throw an error if the color pair number was too large.

`attr-get`   [Procedure]
> The routine `attr-get` returns the current attribute and color pair for the given window. They are returned as a list containing two elements. The first element is a bitmap containing all the attributes. The second element is the color pair alone.

`chgat` *win n attr color #:key y x*   [Procedure]
> The routine `chgat` changes the attributes of a given number of characters starting at the current cursor location of `stdscr` or of *win* if it is given. It does not update the cursor and does not perform wrapping. A character count of -1 or greater than the remaining window width means to change attributes all the way to the end of the current line. If *y* and *x* are given, the function does a cursor move before acting. In these functions, the *color* argument is a color-pair index as in the first argument of `init-pair!`. See Section 5.2.13 [Color manipulation routines], page 69.
>
> The return value is unspecified.

The attributes can be passed to the routines `attr-on!`, `attr-off!`, and `attr-set!`, or `logior`'d with the characters passed to `addch`. For the color part of the rendition, use `color-pair`. See Table 5.2.

`color-pair` *n*   [Procedure]
> Returns a bit mask to apply the color pair *n* to a rendition. `color-pair` values can only be `logior`'ed with attributes if the pair number is less than 256. The alternate functions such as `color-set!` can pass a color pair value directly.

For example, the following two calls are equivalent ways of setting the default attribute of the screen to be bold and have color-pair #1.

> `(attr-set! win (logior A_BOLD (color-pair 1)))`

or

> `(attr-set! win A_BOLD 1)`

`pair-number` *attrs*   [Procedure]
> This function is the inverse operation of `color-pair`. It is rarely useful.
>
> `(color-pair 1) ==> 256`
> `(pair-number 256) ==> 1`

Name	Description
A_NORMAL	Normal display (no highlight)
A_STANDOUT	Best highlighting mode of the terminal.
A_UNDERLINE	Underlining
A_REVERSE	Reverse video
A_BLINK	Blinking
A_DIM	Half bright
A_BOLD	Extra bright or bold
A_PROTECT	Protected mode
A_INVIS	Invisible or blank mode
A_ALTCHARSET	Alternate character set
A_CHARTEXT	Bit-mask to extract a character

Table 5.2: Attributes

5.2.9 Bell and screen flash routines

`beep`   [Procedure]
`flash`   [Procedure]

The `beep` and `flash` routines are used to alert the terminal user. The routine beep sounds an audible alarm on the terminal, if possible; otherwise it flashes the screen (visible bell). The routine flash flashes the screen, and if that is not possible, sounds the alert. If neither alert is possible, nothing happens. Nearly all terminals have an audible alert (bell or beep), but only some can flash the screen.

These routines return #t if they succeed in beeping or flashing, #f otherwise.

5.2.10 Window background manipulation routines

`bkgdset!` *win ch*   [Procedure]

The `bkgdset!` routine manipulates the background of the named window. The window background is set to the rendered complex character *ch*. The attribute part of the *ch* is combined (`logior`'d) with all non-blank characters that are written into the window with `addch`. Both the character and attribute parts of the *ch* are combined with the blank characters. The background becomes a property of the character and moves with the character through any scrolling and insert/delete line/character operations.

To the extent possible on a particular terminal, the attribute part of the background is displayed as the graphic rendition of the character put on the screen.

The return value is undefined.

bkgd *win ch*   [Procedure]

The **bkgd** function sets the background property of the current or specified window and then applies this setting to every character position in that window: The rendition of every character on the screen is changed to the new background rendition. Wherever the former background character appears, it is changed to the new background character.

The return value is undefined.

getbkgd *win*   [Procedure]

The **getbkgd** function returns the given window's current background rendered character.

5.2.11 Borders and lines

border *win ls rs ts bs tl tr bl br*   [Procedure]

The **border** routine draws a box around the edges of a window. Other than *win*, each argument is a rendered character, representing a side or a corner of the border. The arguments are *ls* - left side, *rs* - right side, *ts* - top side, *bs* - bottom side, *tl* - top left-hand corner, *tr* - top right-hand corner, *bl* - bottom left-hand corner, and *br* - bottom right-hand corner.

If any of these arguments is zero, then the corresponding default values are used instead. The default values are the line drawing characters that create a box, and they would be *ls* = **acs-vline**, *rs* = **acs-vline**, *ts* = **acs-hline**, *bs* = **acs-hline**, *tl* = **acs-ulcorner**, *tr* = **acs-urcorner**, *bl* = **acs-llcorner**, *br* = **acs-lrcorner**.

The characters used should have the standard character width. Double-width characters should not be used in borders.

It returns **#f** on failure and **#t** on success.

box *win verch horch*   [Procedure]

box is a shorthand for the following call:

```
(border win verch verch horch horch 0 0 0 0)
```

hline *win ch n #:key y x*   [Procedure]

The **hline** procedure draws a horizontal (left to right) line using *ch* starting at the current cursor position in the window. The current cursor position is not changed. The line is at most *n* characters long, or as many as fit into the window.

The optional parameters *y* and *x* cause the cursor to be moved to that position before drawing the line.

The return value is unspecified.

`vline` *win ch n #:key y x*   [Procedure]

>   The `vline` procedure draws a vertical (top to bottom) line using `ch` starting at the
>   current cursor position in the window. The current cursor position is not changed.
>   The line is at most `n` characters long, or as many as fit into the window.
>
>   If the key parameters *y* and *x* are set, it moves the cursor before drawing the line.
>
>   The return value is unspecified.

5.2.12 Clearing windows and parts of window

The following family of functions *clear* all or part of a window. When clearing a window,
the blanks created by erasure have the current background rendition (as set by `bkgdset!`)
merged into them.

`erase` *win*   [Procedure]

>   The `erase` routine copies blanks to every position in the window, clearing the screen.
>
>   It returns `#f` on failure and `#t` on success.

`clear` *win*   [Procedure]

>   The `clear` routine is like `erase`, but they also call `clearok!`, so that the screen is
>   cleared completely on the next call to `refresh` for that window and repainted from
>   scratch.
>
>   Its return value is unspecified.

`clrtobot` *win*   [Procedure]

>   The `clrtobot` routine erase from the cursor to the end of screen. That is, they erase
>   all lines below the cursor in the window. Also, the current line to the right of the
>   cursor, inclusive, is erased.
>
>   Its return value is unspecified.

`clrtoeol` *win*   [Procedure]

>   The `clrtoeol` routine erase the current line to the right of the cursor, inclusive, to
>   the end of the current line.
>
>   It returns `#f` on failure and `#t` on success. Failure could occur if the cursor position
>   is offscreen.

5.2.13 Color manipulation routines

Curses supports color attributes on terminals with that capability. To use these routines
`start-color!` must be called, usually right after `initscr`. Colors are always used in pairs
(referred to as color-pairs). A color-pair consists of a foreground color (for characters) and a
background color (for the blank field on which the characters are displayed). A programmer
initializes a color-pair with the routine `init-pair!`. After it has been initialized, `color-pair` can be used as a new video attribute.

If a terminal is capable of redefining colors, the programmer can use the routine `init-color!` to change the definition of a color. The routines `has-colors?` and `can-change-color?` return `#t` or `#f`, depending on whether the terminal has color capabilities and
whether the programmer can change the colors. The routine `color-content` allows a
programmer to extract the amounts of red, green, and blue components in an initialized
color. The routine `pair-content` allows a programmer to find out how a given color-pair
is currently defined.

start-color! [Procedure]

> The **start-color!** routine requires no arguments. It must be called if the programmer wants to use colors, and before any other color manipulation routine is called. It is good practice to call this routine right after **initscr**. **start-color!** initializes eight basic colors (black, red, green, yellow, blue, magenta, cyan, and white), and prepares the procedures **colors** and **color-pairs** (respectively defining the maximum number of colors and color-pairs the terminal can support). It also restores the colors on the terminal to the values they had when the terminal was just turned on.
>
> The return value is unspecified.

colors [Procedure]

> Returns the maximum number of colors the terminal can support.

color-pairs [Procedure]

> Returns the maximum number of color-pairs the terminal can support.

COLOR_BLACK	[Constant]
COLOR_RED	[Constant]
COLOR_GREEN	[Constant]
COLOR_YELLOW	[Constant]
COLOR_BLUE	[Constant]
COLOR_MAGENTA	[Constant]
COLOR_CYAN	[Constant]
COLOR_WHITE	[Constant]

> These variables contain the color number of the eight default colors.

init-color! *color red green blue* [Procedure]

> The **init-color!** routine changes the definition of a color. It takes four arguments: the number of the color to be changed followed by three RGB values (for the amounts of *red*, *green*, and *blue* components). The value of the first argument must be between 0 and the value returned by the **colors** procedure. Each of the last three arguments must be a value between 0 and 1000. When **init-color!** is used, all occurrences of that color on the screen immediately change to the new definition.
>
> It returns #f on failure and #t on success. Failure may indicate that, for the current terminal, the colors cannot be modified.

init-pair! *color-pair fore-color back-color* [Procedure]

> The **init-pair!** routine changes the definition of a color-pair. It takes three arguments: the number of the color-pair to be changed, the fore-ground color number, and the background color number.
>
> The value of the first argument must be between 1 and **color-pairs** - 1.
>
> The value of the second and third arguments must be between 0 and **colors**. Color pair 0 is assumed to be white on black, but is actually whatever the terminal implements before color is initialized.
>
> If the color-pair was previously initialized, the screen is refreshed and all occurrences of that color-pair are changed to the new definition.
>
> Color pair 0 is set via the **assume-default-colors** routine. After **use-default-colors** has been called, the special color number -1 can be

used as *fore-color* or *back-color*. Color number -1 is set to contain the default foreground or background color for this screen, which is usually white on black.

It returns #f on failure and #t on success. Failure may indicate an attempt to change a color pair beyond the allow range of color pairs.

has-colors?   [Procedure]

The has-colors? routine returns #t if the terminal can manipulate colors; otherwise, it returns #f. This routine facilitates writing terminal-independent programs. For example, a programmer can use it to decide whether to use color or some other video attribute.

can-change-color?   [Procedure]

The can-change-color? routine returns #t if the terminal supports colors and can change their definitions; otherwise, it returns #f.

color-content *color*   [Procedure]

The color-content routine returns the intensity of the red, green, and blue (RGB) components in a color. Given *color* as its argument, it returns a list of three integers indicating the red, green, and blue components in the given color. The value of the *color* argument must be between 0 and the value returned by the colors procedure. The values returned are between 0 (no component) and 1000 (maximum amount of component).

pair-content *pair*   [Procedure]

The pair-content routine allows programmers to find out what colors color-pair *pair* consists of. The value of *pair* must be between 1 and color-pairs - 1. It returns a list of two elements: the foreground color number and the background color number. The values are between 0 and the value returned by colors.

use-default-colors   [Procedure]

This procedure allow routines that use color numbers, like init-pair! to use the special color number -1 to indicate the default color. When -1 is used in lieu of the foreground color, it indicated the default foreground color. When -1 is used as the background color, it indicated the default background color. Thus, it has different meanings depending on the context.

It returns #t if successful or #f is the terminal lacks the capability to set color pair 0.

assume-default-colors *fg bg*   [Procedure]

This procedure allow the modification of special color pair 0, which cannot be modified by init-pair!. Color pair 0 is the default foreground and background color for the window.

It returns #t if successful or #f is the terminal lacks the capability to set color pair 0.

5.2.14 Deleting the character under the cursor

delch *win #:key y x*   [Procedure]

This routine deletes the character under the cursor; all characters to the right of the cursor on the same line are moved to the left one position and the last character on the line is filled with a blank. The cursor position does not change (after moving to y, x, if specified). (This does not imply use of the hardware delete character feature.)

It returns **#f** on failure and **#t** on success.

5.2.15 Deleting and inserting lines

deleteln *win*   [Procedure]

The **deleteln** procedure deletes the line under the cursor in the window; all lines below the current line are moved up one line. The bottom line of the window is cleared. The cursor position does not change.

It returns **#f** on failure and **#t** on success.

insdelln *win n*   [Procedure]

The **insdelln** routine, for positive *n*, inserts *n* lines into the specified window above the current line. The *n* bottom lines are lost. For negative *n*, it deletes n lines (starting with the one under the cursor), and move the remaining lines up. The bottom n lines are cleared. The current cursor position remains the same.

It returns **#f** on failure and **#t** on success.

insertln *win*   [Procedure]

The **insertln** routine inserts a blank line above the current line and the bottom line is lost.

It returns **#f** on failure and **#t** on success.

5.2.16 Getting characters from the keyboard

getch *win #:key y x*   [Procedure]

The **getch** routine reads a character from the terminal associated with the given window. In no-delay mode, if no input is waiting, the value **#f** is returned. In delay mode, the program waits until the system passes text through to the program. Depending on the setting of cbreak, this is after one character (**cbreak** mode), or after the first newline (**nocbreak!** mode). In **halfdelay!** mode, the program waits until a character is typed or the specified timeout has been reached.

Unless **noecho!** has been set, then the character will also be echoed into the designated window according to the following rules: If the character is the current erase character, left arrow, or backspace, the cursor is moved one space to the left and that screen position is erased as if **delch** had been called. If the character value is any other **KEY_** define, the user is alerted with a **beep** call. Otherwise the character is simply output to the screen.

If **keypad!** is **#t**, and a function key is pressed, the integer keycode for that function key is returned instead of the raw characters. There is a list of possible function keys. See Table 5.3.

When a character that could be the beginning of a function key is received (which, on modern terminals, means an escape character), curses sets a timer. If the remainder of the sequence does not come in within the designated time, the character is passed through; otherwise, the function key value is returned. For this reason, many terminals experience a delay between the time a user presses the escape key and the escape is returned to the program.

If the window is not a pad, and it has been moved or modified since the last call to `refresh`, `refresh` will be called before another character is read.

ungetch *ch*   [Procedure]

    The ungetch routine places *ch* back onto the input queue to be returned by the next call to `getch`. There is just one input queue for all windows.

    It returns `#f` if there is no more space in the buffer, or `#t` otherwise.

key-f *n*   [Procedure]

    This procedure returns the keycode for function key *n*.

The following function keys, might be returned by `getch` if `keypad!` has been enabled.

Note that almost all of these function keys do not exist on modern keyboards. The standard PC keyboard cannot be depended upon to have more than (`key-f 1`) through (`key-f 12`), `KEY_PPAGE` (Page Up), `KEY_NPAGE` (Page Down), `KEY_HOME`, `KEY_END`, `KEY_IC` (Insert), `KEY_DC` (Delete), `KEY_BACKSPACE`, `KEY_DC` (Delete), `KEY_UP`, `KEY_DOWN`, `KEY_LEFT`, and `KEY_RIGHT`.

Also, a common terminal is more likely to return *C-M* than `KEY_ENTER` when the `RET` key is pressed.

name	description
KEY_BREAK	Break key
KEY_DOWN	Arrow down
KEY_UP	Arrow up
KEY_LEFT	Arrow left
KEY_RIGHT	Arrow right
KEY_HOME	Home key
KEY_BACKSPACE	Backspace
KEY_F0	Function key zero
KEY_DL	Delete line
KEY_IL	Insert line
KEY_DC	Delete character
KEY_IC	Insert char or enter insert mode
KEY_EIC	Exit insert char mode
KEY_CLEAR	Clear screen
KEY_EOS	Clear to end of screen
KEY_EOL	Clear to end of line
KEY_SF	Scroll 1 line forward
KEY_SR	Scroll 1 line backward (reverse)
KEY_NPAGE	Next page
KEY_PPAGE	Previous page
KEY_STAB	Set tab
KEY_CTAB	Clear tab
KEY_CATAB	Clear all tabs
KEY_ENTER	Enter or send
KEY_SRESET	Soft (partial) reset
KEY_RESET	Reset or hard reset
KEY_PRINT	Print or copy
KEY_LL	Home down or bottom (lower left)
KEY_A1	Upper left of keypad
KEY_A3	Upper right of keypad
KEY_B2	Center of keypad
KEY_C1	Lower left of keypad
KEY_C3	Lower right of keypad
KEY_BTAB	Back tab key
KEY_BEG	Beg(inning) key
KEY_CANCEL	Cancel key
KEY_CLOSE	Close key
KEY_COMMAND	Cmd (command) key
KEY_COPY	Copy key
KEY_CREATE	Create key
KEY_END	End key
KEY_EXIT	Exit key
KEY_FIND	Find key
KEY_HELP	Help key
KEY_MARK	Mark key
KEY_MESSAGE	Message key

Table 5.3: the keypad constants, part 1

name	description
KEY_MOUSE	Mouse event read
KEY_MOVE	Move key
KEY_NEXT	Next object key
KEY_OPEN	Open key
KEY_OPTIONS	Options key
KEY_PREVIOUS	Previous object key
KEY_REDO	Redo key
KEY_REFERENCE	Ref(erence) key
KEY_REFRESH	Refresh key
KEY_REPLACE	Replace key
KEY_RESIZE	Screen resized
KEY_RESTART	Restart key
KEY_RESUME	Resume key
KEY_SAVE	Save key
KEY_SBEG	Shifted beginning key
KEY_SCANCEL	Shifted cancel key
KEY_SCOMMAND	Shifted command key
KEY_SCOPY	Shifted copy key
KEY_SCREATE	Shifted create key
KEY_SDC	Shifted delete char key
KEY_SDL	Shifted delete line key
KEY_SELECT	Select key
KEY_SEND	Shifted end key
KEY_SEOL	Shifted clear line key
KEY_SEXIT	Shifted exit key
KEY_SFIND	Shifted find key
KEY_SHELP	Shifted help key
KEY_SHOME	Shifted home key
KEY_SIC	Shifted input key
KEY_SLEFT	Shifted left arrow key
KEY_SMESSAGE	Shifted message key
KEY_SMOVE	Shifted move key
KEY_SNEXT	Shifted next key
KEY_SOPTIONS	Shifted options key
KEY_SPREVIOUS	Shifted prev key
KEY_SPRINT	Shifted print key
KEY_SREDO	Shifted redo key
KEY_SREPLACE	Shifted replace key
KEY_SRIGHT	Shifted right arrow
KEY_SRESUME	Shifted resume key
KEY_SSAVE	Shifted save key
KEY_SSUSPEND	Shifted suspend key
KEY_SUNDO	Shifted undo key
KEY_SUSPEND	Suspend key
KEY_UNDO	Undo key

Table 5.4: the keypad constants, part 2

`has-key?` *ch*   [Procedure]

> The `has-key?` routine takes a key value *ch* from the above list, and returns `#t` or `#f` according to whether the current terminal type recognizes a key with that value. Note that a few values do not correspond to a real key, e.g., `KEY_RESIZE` and `KEY_MOUSE`. See `resizeterm` for more details about `KEY_RESIZE`. For a discussion of `KEY_MOUSE` see Section 5.2.27 [Mouse handling], page 82.

Use of the `ESC` key by a programmer for a single character function is discouraged, as it will cause a delay of up to one second while the keypad code looks for a following function-key sequence.

Note that some keys may be the same as commonly used control keys, e.g., KEY_ENTER versus *C-M*, KEY_BACKSPACE versus *C-H*. Some curses implementations may differ according to whether they treat these control keys specially (and ignore the terminfo), or use the terminfo definitions. Ncurses uses the terminfo definition. If it says that KEY_ENTER is *C-M*, `getch` will return KEY_ENTER when you press *C-M*.

When using `getch`, `wgetch`, `mvgetch`, or `mvwgetch`, nocbreak mode (`nocbreak!`) and echo mode (`echo!`) should not be used at the same time. Depending on the state of the TTY driver when each character is typed, the program may produce undesirable results.

Historically, the set of keypad macros was largely defined by the extremely function-key-rich keyboard of the AT&T 7300, aka 3B1, aka Safari 4. Modern personal computers usually have only a small subset of these. IBM PC-style consoles typically support little more than `KEY_UP`, `KEY_DOWN`, `KEY_LEFT`, `KEY_RIGHT`, `KEY_HOME`, `KEY_END`, `KEY_NPAGE`, `KEY_PPAGE`, and function keys 1 through 12. The ins key is usually mapped to `KEY_IC`

5.2.17 Handling unmapped keys

For most every modern-day terminal, you'll find that if you get the `TERM` environment variable set correctly, then each of the function keys on the keyboard will be interpreted as a key code.

But in rare circumstances, you may find that a function key on your keyboard is not being mapped to a keycode. As an example, on some keyboards there is a special "menu" key in between `Ctrl` and `Alt`. On my keyboard, pressing "menu" returns "ESC [2 9 ~", which `getch` returns as a that 5 separate characters, instead of a single keycode like `KEY_MENU`.

When this happens, the problem is most often that you've set your `TERM` incorrectly. Next most likely is that your terminfo or termcap database is out of date. That is where you should first seek your solution.

But, if that fails, and you need a quick-and-dirty workaround, `define-key` can help. It lets you map an escape sequence to a key code.

Continuing my example, if I choose to map this menu key to a keycode, I can choose the keycode of a key that that doesn't appear on my keyboard, like `KEY_FIND`, and associate with that string, using `define-key`.

`define-key` *defn keycode*   [Procedure]

> This procedure defines a new, custom *keycode*. When the string in *defn* is input, routines like `getch` will return the keycode instead, if the keypad is on. If *defn* is an empty string, the keycode will be cleared.

If *keycode* is an existing keycode, its *defn* replaces its previous definition.

The return value is #t on success.

For the example, I can use the command

```
(define-key (string #\esc #\[ #\2 #\9 #\~) KEY_FIND)
```

From that point on, when the Menu key is pressed, getch will return the integer KEY_FIND.

key-defined *defn*   [Procedure]

If the string *defn* is a character sequence that is bound to a keycode, that keycode is returned. Otherwise #f is returned.

5.2.18 Receiving strings from the keyboard

getnstr *win n #:key y x*   [Procedure]

The procedure getnstr is equivalent to a series of calls to getch, until a newline or carriage return is received (the terminating character is not included in the returned string). The resulting string is returned.

getnstr reads at most *n* characters, thus preventing a possible overflow of the input buffer. Any attempt to enter more characters (other than the terminating newline or carriage return) causes a beep. Function keys also cause a beep and are ignored.

The user's erase and kill characters are interpreted. If keypad mode is on for the window, KEY_LEFT and KEY_BACKSPACE are both considered equivalent to the user's kill character.

Characters input are echoed only if echo! is currently on. In that case, backspace is echoed as deletion of the previous character (typically a left motion).

If a SIGWINCH interrupts the function, it will return the integer value of KEY_RESIZE instead of a string.

5.2.19 Cursor location and window coordinates

getyx *win*   [Procedure]
getcurx *win*   [Procedure]
getcury *win*   [Procedure]

The getyx procedure returns the current cursor position as a list containing two integers. The first is the y position and the second is the x position.

The other two procedures return the x y positions respectively.

getparyx *win*   [Procedure]
getparx *win*   [Procedure]
getpary *win*   [Procedure]

If *win* is a subwindow, the getparyx procedure places the beginning coordinates of the subwindow relative to the parent window into two element list (y x). Otherwise, (-1 -1) is returned.

The other two procedures return the x and y respectively.

getbegyx *win* [Procedure]
getbegx *win* [Procedure]
getbegy *win* [Procedure]
> The procedure `getbegyx` returns the beginning coordinates of a window as two element list (y x).

getmaxyx *win* [Procedure]
getmaxx *win* [Procedure]
getmaxy *win* [Procedure]
> The procedure `getmaxyx` returns the size of a window as two element list (y x).

5.2.20 Getting a rendered character from the window

These functions examine a character on the screen and return it, along with its rendition.

inch [Procedure]
> These routines return the rendered complex character at the current position in the named window.

5.2.21 Getting a string of characters and attributes from a window

inchnstr *win #:key y x n* [Procedure]
> These routines return a list of rendered characters, starting at the current cursor position in the named window and ending at the right margin of the window or until *n* characters have been found.

5.2.22 Input options

cbreak! [Procedure]
nocbreak! [Procedure]
> Normally, the TTY driver buffers typed characters until a NL or RET is typed. The `cbreak!` routine disables line buffering and erase/kill character processing (interrupt and flow control characters are unaffected), making characters typed by the user immediately available to the program.
>
> The `nocbreak!` routine returns the terminal to normal (cooked) mode.
>
> These routines will return #t on success and #f on failure. Failure may indicate that the underlying screen data is invalid. The routine may also fail if `cbreak!` was called on an ordinary file (such as might be used with `newterm`) instead of a TTY.
>
> Initially the terminal may or may not be in `cbreak` mode, as the mode is inherited; therefore, a program should call `cbreak!` or `nocbreak!` explicitly. Most interactive programs using curses set the `cbreak!` mode. Note that `cbreak!` overrides `raw!`.

echo! [Procedure]
noecho! [Procedure]
> The `echo!` and `noecho!` routines control whether characters typed by the user are echoed by getch as they are typed. Echoing by the TTY driver is always disabled, but initially `getch` is in echo mode, so characters typed are echoed. Authors of most interactive programs prefer to do their own echoing in a controlled area of the screen,

or not to echo at all, so they disable echoing by calling `noecho!`. See Section 5.2.16 [Getting characters from the keyboard], page 72 for a discussion of how these routines interact with `echo!` and `noecho!`.

The return values are unspecified.

`halfdelay!` *tenths*   [Procedure]

The `halfdelay!` routine is used for half-delay mode, which is similar to `cbreak!` mode in that characters typed by the user are immediately available to the program. However, after blocking for *tenths* tenths of seconds, `#f` is returned if nothing has been typed. The value of tenths must be a number between 1 and 255. Use `nocbreak!` to leave half-delay mode.

The return value is unspecified.

`intrflush!` *bf*   [Procedure]

If the intrflush option is enabled, (*bf* is `#t`), when an interrupt key is pressed on the keyboard (interrupt, break, quit) all output in the TTY driver queue will be flushed, giving the effect of faster response to the interrupt, but causing curses to have the wrong idea of what is on the screen. Disabling (*bf* is `#f`), the option prevents the flush. The default for the option is inherited from the TTY driver settings.

The return value is unspecified.

`keypad!` *win bf*   [Procedure]

The `keypad!` option enables the keypad of the user's terminal. If enabled (*bf* is `#t`), the user can press a function key (such as an arrow key) and `getch` returns a single value representing the function key, as in `KEY_LEFT`. If disabled (*bf* is `#f`), curses does not treat function keys specially and the program has to interpret the escape sequences itself. If the keypad in the terminal can be turned on (made to transmit) and off (made to work locally), turning on this option causes the terminal keypad to be turned on when `getch` is called. The default value for keypad is `#f`.

The return value is unspecified. This procedure could throw a "bad state" error.

`meta!` *bf*   [Procedure]

If Guile-Ncurses was compiled with the standard version of the ncurses library, and not the wide version, it operates on 8-bit characters.

Initially, whether the terminal returns 7 or 8 significant bits on input depends on the control mode of the TTY driver. To force 8 bits to be returned, invoke (`meta!` `#t`). This is equivalent, under POSIX, to setting the CS8 flag on the terminal. To force 7 bits to be returned, invoke (`meta!` `#f`). This is equivalent, under POSIX, to setting the CS7 flag on the terminal. The window argument, *win*, is always ignored. If the terminfo capabilities `smm` (meta-on) and `rmm` (meta-off) are defined for the terminal. The code for `smm` is sent to the terminal when (`meta!` `#t`) is called and `rmm` is sent when (`meta!` `#f`) is called.

The return value is unspecified.

`nodelay!` *win bf*   [Procedure]

The `nodelay!` option causes `getch` to be a non-blocking call. If no input is ready, getch returns `#f`. If disabled (*bf* is `#f`), `getch` waits until a key is pressed.

The return value is unspecified.

notimeout! *win bf*   [Procedure]

> While interpreting an input escape sequence, `getch` sets a timer while waiting for the next character. If (`notimeout! win #t`) is called, then `getch` does not set a timer. The purpose of the timeout is to differentiate between sequences received from a function key and those typed by a user.
>
> The return value is unspecified.

raw!   [Procedure]
noraw!   [Procedure]

> The `raw!` and `noraw!` routines place the terminal into or out of raw mode. Raw mode is similar to `cbreak!` mode, in that characters typed are immediately passed through to the user program. The differences are that in raw mode, the interrupt, quit, suspend, and flow control characters are all passed through uninterpreted, instead of generating a signal. The behavior of the **BREAK** key depends on other bits in the TTY driver that are not set by curses.
>
> The return value is unspecified.

noqiflush!   [Procedure]
qiflush!   [Procedure]

> When the `noqiflush!` routine is used, normal flush of input and output queues associated with the INTR, QUIT and SUSP characters will not be done. When `qiflush!` is called, the queues will be flushed when these control characters are read. You may want to call `noqiflush!` in a signal handler if you want output to continue as though the interrupt had not occurred, after the handler exits.
>
> The return value is unspecified.

timeout! *win delay*   [Procedure]

> The `timeout!` routine sets blocking or non-blocking read for a given window. If *delay* is negative, blocking read is used (i.e., waits indefinitely for input). If *delay* is zero, then non-blocking read is used (i.e., read returns `#f` if no input is waiting). If *delay* is positive, then read blocks for delay milliseconds, and returns `#f` if there is still no input. Hence, these routines provide the same functionality as `nodelay!`, plus the additional capability of being able to block for only *delay* milliseconds (where *delay* is positive).

typeahead! *fd*   [Procedure]

> The curses library does "line-breakout optimization" by looking for typeahead periodically while updating the screen. If input is found, and it is coming from a TTY, the current update is postponed until refresh or doupdate is called again. This allows faster response to commands typed in advance. Normally, the input file port passed to newterm, or `stdin` in the case that initscr was used, will be used to do this typeahead checking. The `typeahead!` routine specifies that the (integer) file descriptor *fd* is to be used to check for typeahead instead. If *fd* is -1, then no typeahead checking is done.
>
> The routine returns `#t` if the mode could be set and `#f` on failure.

There are a set of procedures to test the input options of a given window.

```
is-keypad? win                                                        [Procedure]
is-meta? win                                                          [Procedure]
is-nodelay? win                                                       [Procedure]
is-immedok? win                                                       [Procedure]
is-notimeout? win                                                     [Procedure]
```
These test the input options of the window *win* and return **#t** if they are set.

5.2.23 Inserting a character before the cursor

insch *win ch #:key y x*   [Procedure]
These routines insert the character *ch* before the character under the cursor. All characters to the right of the cursor are moved one space to the right, with the possibility of the rightmost character on the line being lost. The insertion operation does not change the cursor position.

It returns **#f** upon failure and **#t** upon successful completion.

5.2.24 Inserting a string before the cursor

insstr *win str #:key y x n*   [Procedure]
This routine inserts a character string (as many characters as will fit on the line) before the character under the cursor. All characters to the right of the cursor are shifted right with the possibility of the rightmost characters on the line being lost. The cursor position does not change (after moving to *y*, *x*, if specified). If *n* is specified, it inserts a leading substring of at most n characters, or if *n*<=0, then the entire string is inserted.

Special characters are handled as in **addch**.

It returns **#f** upon failure and **#t** upon successful completion.

5.2.25 Getting a string of characters from the screen

instr *win #:key y x n*   [Procedure]
This routine returns a unrendered string, extracted starting at the current cursor position in the named window. Attributes are stripped from the characters. If *n* is specified, it returns a leading substring at most *n* characters long.

5.2.26 Low-level routines

The following routines give low-level access to various curses capabilities. Theses routines typically are used inside library routines.

def-prog-mode   [Procedure]
def-shell-mode   [Procedure]
The **def-prog-mode** and **def-shell-mode** routines save the current terminal modes as the "program" (in curses) or "shell" (not in curses) state for use by the **reset-prog-mode** and **reset-shell-mode** routines. This is done automatically by **initscr**. There is one such save area for each screen context allocated by **newterm**.

They return **#t** on success and **#f** on failure.

reset-prog-mode   [Procedure]
reset-shell-mode   [Procedure]
>   The **reset-prog-mode** and **reset-shell-mode** routines restore the terminal to "program" (in curses) or "shell" (out of curses) state. These are done automatically by **endwin** and, after an **endwin**, by **doupdate**, so they normally are not called.
>
>   Returns **#t** on success or **#f** on failure. Failure could indicate that this terminal was created with **newterm** and thus doesn't have a previous state.

resetty   [Procedure]
savetty   [Procedure]
>   The **resetty** and **savetty** routines save and restore the state of the terminal modes. **savetty** saves the current state in a buffer and **resetty** restores the state to what it was at the last call to **savetty**.
>
>   Returns **#t** on success or **#f** on failure. Failure could indicate that this terminal was created with **newterm** and thus doesn't have a previous state.

curs-set *visibility*   [Procedure]
>   The **curs-set** routine changes the visibility of the cursor. If *visibility* is 0, the cursor is set to invisible. For 1, the cursor is visible. For 2, the cursor is very visible. If the terminal supports the visibility requested, the previous cursor state is returned; otherwise, **#f** is returned.

napms *ms*   [Procedure]
>   The procedure is used to sleep for *ms* milliseconds.
>
>   The return value is unspecified.

5.2.27 Mouse handling

These functions provide an interface to mouse events. Mouse events are represented by **KEY_MOUSE** pseudo-key values in the **wgetch** input stream.

>   To make mouse events visible, use the **mousemask** function.

has-mouse?   [Procedure]
>   Returns **#t** if the mouse driver has been successfully installed.

mousemask *mask*   [Procedure]
>   This will set the mouse events to be reported. By default, no mouse events are reported. The function will return a mask to indicate which of the specified mouse events can be reported; on complete failure it returns 0.
>
>   As a side effect, setting a zero mousemask may turn off the mouse pointer; setting a nonzero mask may turn it on. Whether this happens is device-dependent.
>
>   See Table 5.5 for the mouse event types mask that may be defined.

name	description
BUTTON1_PRESSED	mouse button 1 down
BUTTON1_RELEASED	mouse button 1 up
BUTTON1_CLICKED	mouse button 1 clicked
BUTTON1_DOUBLE_CLICKED	mouse button 1 double clicked
BUTTON1_TRIPLE_CLICKED	mouse button 1 triple clicked
BUTTON2_PRESSED	mouse button 2 down
BUTTON2_RELEASED	mouse button 2 up
BUTTON2_CLICKED	mouse button 2 clicked
BUTTON2_DOUBLE_CLICKED	mouse button 2 double clicked
BUTTON2_TRIPLE_CLICKED	mouse button 2 triple clicked
BUTTON3_PRESSED	mouse button 3 down
BUTTON3_RELEASED	mouse button 3 up
BUTTON3_CLICKED	mouse button 3 clicked
BUTTON3_DOUBLE_CLICKED	mouse button 3 double clicked
BUTTON3_TRIPLE_CLICKED	mouse button 3 triple clicked
BUTTON4_PRESSED	mouse button 4 down
BUTTON4_RELEASED	mouse button 4 up
BUTTON4_CLICKED	mouse button 4 clicked
BUTTON4_DOUBLE_CLICKED	mouse button 4 double clicked
BUTTON4_TRIPLE_CLICKED	mouse button 4 triple clicked
BUTTON5_PRESSED	mouse button 5 down
BUTTON5_RELEASED	mouse button 5 up
BUTTON5_CLICKED	mouse button 5 clicked
BUTTON5_DOUBLE_CLICKED	mouse button 5 double clicked
BUTTON5_TRIPLE_CLICKED	mouse button 5 triple clicked
BUTTON_SHIFT	shift was down during button state change
BUTTON_CTRL	control was down during button state change
BUTTON_ALT	alt was down during button state change
ALL_MOUSE_EVENTS	report all button state changes
REPORT_MOUSE_POSITION	report mouse movement

Table 5.5: Mouse mask constants

Once a class of mouse events have been made visible in a window, calling the wgetch function on that window may return KEY_MOUSE as an indicator that a mouse event has been queued. To read the event data and pop the event off the queue, call getmouse.

getmouse   [Procedure]
    This will return either a list of mouse information, or #f. If it does return a list, it
    will have the following form:

```
(id                   ; id to distinguish multiple devices
 x y z                ; event coordinates
 bstate)              ; button state bits
```

When `getmouse` returns a list, the data deposited as y and x in the list will be screen-relative character-cell coordinates. The returned state mask will have exactly one bit set to indicate the event type.

ungetmouse *mouse-event*   [Procedure]

The `ungetmouse` function behaves analogously to `ungetch`. It pushes a `KEY_MOUSE` event onto the input queue, and associates with that event the given state data and screen-relative character-cell coordinates in the *mouse-event* list, where *mouse-event* is a list of five elements as described above.

mouse-trafo *win y x to-screen*   [Procedure]

The `mouse-trafo` function transforms a given pair of coordinates *y, x* from `stdscr`-relative coordinates to coordinates relative to the given window *win* or vice versa. Please remember, that `stdscr`-relative coordinates are not always identical to window-relative coordinates due to the mechanism to reserve lines on top or bottom of the screen for other purposes (see `slk-init`, for example). If the parameter *to-screen* is `#t`, the procedure returns either a list of two elements (y, x) which is the location inside the window *win*, or `#f` if the location was not inside the window. If *to-screen* is `#f`, the return a list of two elements of where the window-relative location *y, x* would be in stdscr-relative coordinates.

The `mouse-trafo` procedure performs the same translation as `wmouse-trafo`, using `stdscr` for *win*.

wenclose? *win y x*   [Procedure]

The `wenclose?` function tests whether a given pair of screen-relative character-cell coordinates is enclosed by the given window *win*, returning `#t` if it is and `#f` otherwise. It is useful for determining what subset of the screen windows enclose the location of a mouse event.

mouseinterval *erval*   [Procedure]

The `mouseinterval` function sets the maximum time (in thousands of a second) that can elapse between press and release events for them to be recognized as a click. Use `(mouseinterval 0)` to disable click resolution. This function returns the previous interval value. Use `(mouseinterval -1)` to obtain the interval without altering it. The default is one sixth of a second.

5.2.28 Moving the cursor

move *win y x*   [Procedure]

This routine moves the cursor associated with the window to line *y* and column *x*. This routine does not move the physical cursor of the terminal until `refresh` is called. The position specified is relative to the upper left-hand corner of the window, which is (0 0).

It returns `#f` upon failure and `#t` on successful completion.

5.2.29 Output options

These routines set options that change the style of output within curses. All options are initially `#f`, unless otherwise stated. It is not necessary to turn these options off before calling `endwin`.

clearok! *win bf*   [Procedure]

If `clearok!` is called with *bf* as `#t`, the next call to `refresh` with this window will clear the screen completely and redraw the entire screen from scratch. This is useful when the contents of the screen are uncertain, or in some cases for a more pleasing visual effect.

The return value is unspecified.

idlok! *win bf*   [Procedure]

If `idlok!` is called with `#t` as second argument, curses considers using the hardware insert/delete line feature of terminals so equipped. Calling `idlok!` with *bf* as `#f` disables use of line insertion and deletion. This option should be enabled only if the application needs insert/delete line, for example, for a screen editor. It is disabled by default because insert/delete line tends to be visually annoying when used in applications where it isn't really needed. If insert/delete line cannot be used, curses redraws the changed portions of all lines.

The return value is unspecified.

idcok! *win bf*   [Procedure]

If `idcok!` is called with *bf* as `#f`, curses no longer considers using the hardware insert/delete character feature of terminals so equipped. Use of character insert/delete is enabled by default. Calling `idcok!` with `#t` as second argument re-enables use of character insertion and deletion.

The return value is unspecified.

immedok! *win bf*   [Procedure]

If `immedok!` is called with `#t` as argument, any change in the window image, such as the ones caused by `addch`, `clrtobot`, `scrl`, etc., automatically cause a call to `refresh`. However, it may degrade performance considerably, due to repeated calls to `refresh`. It is disabled by default.

The return value is unspecified.

leaveok! *win bf*   [Procedure]

Normally, the hardware cursor is left at the location of the window cursor being refreshed. The `leaveok!` option allows the cursor to be left wherever the update happens to leave it. It is useful for applications where the cursor is not used, since it reduces the need for cursor motions.

setscrreg! *win top bot*   [Procedure]

The `setscrreg!` routine allows the application programmer to set a software scrolling region in a window. *top* and *bot* are the line numbers of the top and bottom margin of the scrolling region. (Line 0 is the top line of the window.) If this option and `scrollok!` are enabled, an attempt to move off the bottom margin line causes all lines in the scrolling region to scroll one line in the direction of the first line. Only the text of the window is scrolled. (Note that this has nothing to do with the use of a physical scrolling region capability in the terminal, like that in the VT100. If `idlok!` is enabled and the terminal has either a scrolling region or insert/delete line capability, they will probably be used by the output routines.)

getscrreg *win*   [Procedure]

> Returns a two-element list that contains the line numbers of the top and bottom of the scroll region for the window *win*.

scrollok! *win bf*   [Procedure]

> The **scrollok!** option controls what happens when the cursor of a window is moved off the edge of the window or scrolling region, either as a result of a newline action on the bottom line, or typing the last character of the last line. If disabled, (*bf* is **#f**), the cursor is left on the bottom line. If enabled, (*bf* is **#t**), the window is scrolled up one line (Note that to get the physical scrolling effect on the terminal, it is also necessary to call **idlok!**).
>
> The return value is unspecified.

nl!   [Procedure]
nonl!   [Procedure]

> The **nl!** and **nonl!** routines control whether the underlying display device translates RET (return) into NL (newline) on input, and whether it translates NL into RET and LF (linefeed) output (in either case, the call (**addch (normal #\nl)**) does the equivalent of return and line feed on the virtual screen). Initially, these translations do occur. If you disable them using **nonl!**, curses will be able to make better use of the line-feed capability, resulting in faster cursor motion. Also, curses will then be able to detect the return key.
>
> The return values are unspecified;

There are a set of procedures to test the output options of a given window.

is-cleared? *win*   [Procedure]
is-idlok? *win*   [Procedure]
is-idcok? *win*   [Procedure]
is-immedok? *win*   [Procedure]
is-leaveok? *win*   [Procedure]
is-scrollok? *win*   [Procedure]

> These test the output options of the window *win* and return **#t** if they are set.

5.2.30 Overlay and manipulate overlapped windows

overlay *srcwin dstwin*   [Procedure]
overwrite *srcwin dstwin*   [Procedure]

> The **overlay** and **overwrite** routines overlay *srcwin* on top of *dstwin*. *scrwin* and *dstwin* are not required to be the same size; only text where the two windows overlap is copied. The difference is that overlay is non-destructive (blanks are not copied) whereas overwrite is destructive.
>
> The return values are unspecified.

copywin *srcwin dstwin sminrow smincol dminrow dmincol dmaxrow*   [Procedure]
> *dmaxcol overlay*

> The **copywin** routine provides a finer granularity of control over the **overlay** and **overwrite** routines. Like in the **prefresh** routine, a rectangle is specified in the

destination window, (*dminrow*, *dmincol*) and (*dmaxrow*, *dmaxcol*), and the upper-left-corner coordinates of the source window, (*sminrow*, *smincol*). If the argument *overlay* is `#t`, then copying is non-destructive, as in overlay.

Returns `#t` on success or `#f` on failure. `#f` could indicate that some part of the window would be placed offscreen.

5.2.31 Create and display pads

A pad is like a window, except that it is not restricted by the screen size, and is not necessarily associated with a particular part of the screen. Pads can be used when a large window is needed, and only a part of the window will be on the screen at one time. Automatic refreshes of pads (e.g., from scrolling or echoing of input) do not occur. It is not legal to call `refresh` with a pad as an argument; the routines `prefresh` or `pnoutrefresh` should be called instead. Note that these routines require additional parameters to specify the part of the pad to be displayed and the location on the screen to be used for the display.

`newpad` *nlines ncols*   [Procedure]
> The newpad routine creates and returns `#<window>` pad with the given number of lines, *nlines*, and columns, *ncols*.

`is-pad?` *win*   [Procedure]
> Returns `#t` if *win* is a pad. `#f` otherwise.
>
> If the underlying ncurses implementation is not capable of reporting whether a window is a pad, this function will always return `#t`. This can happen in older versions of ncurses that were compiled with the `NCURSES_OPAQUE` option enabled.
>
> To see if this `is-pad?` procedure actually works, you can check the constant `%is-pad-broken`, which will be #f is `is-pad?` actually works.

`subpad` *orig nlines ncols begin-y begin-x*   [Procedure]
> The `subpad` routine creates and returns a pointer to a subwindow within a pad with the given number of lines, *nlines*, and columns, *ncols*. Unlike `subwin`, which uses screen coordinates, the window is at position (*begin-x*, *begin-y*) on the pad. The window is made in the middle of the window orig, so that changes made to one window affect both windows. During the use of this routine, it will often be necessary to call `touchwin` or `touchline` on orig before calling `prefresh`.

`prefresh` *pad pminrow pmincol sminrow simincol smaxrow smaxcol*   [Procedure]
`pnoutrefresh` *pad pminrow pmincol sminrow smincol smaxrow smaxcol*   [Procedure]
> The `prefresh` and `pnoutrefresh` routines are analogous to `refresh` and `noutrefresh` except that they relate to pads instead of windows. The additional parameters are needed to indicate what part of the pad and screen are involved. *pminrow* and `pmincol` specify the upper left-hand corner of the rectangle to be displayed in the pad. *sminrow*, *smincol*, *smaxrow*, and *smaxcol* specify the edges of the rectangle to be displayed on the screen. The lower right-hand corner of the rectangle to be displayed in the pad is calculated from the screen coordinates, since the rectangles must be the same size. Both rectangles must be entirely contained within their respective structures. Negative values of *pminrow*, *pmincol*, *sminrow*, or *smincol* are treated as if they were zero.
>
> Returns `#f` upon failure and `#t` upon successful

pechochar *pad ch*   [Procedure]

>   The `pechochar` routine is functionally equivalent to a call to `addch` followed by a
>   call to `refresh` or a call to `addch` followed by a call to `prefresh`. The knowledge
>   that only a single character is being output is taken into consideration and, for non-
>   control characters, a considerable performance gain might be seen by using these
>   routines instead of their equivalents. In the case of `pechochar`, the last location of
>   the pad on the screen is reused for the arguments to `prefresh`.
>
>   Returns `#f` upon failure and `#t` upon successful completion.

5.2.32 Print data to a terminal-attached ports

Some old-school hardware terminals had serial or parallel ports attached to them. There
is a procedure to send data to those ports. Usually those ports were used for old serial
dot-matrix printers. This function is likely obsolete.

mcprint *str*   [Procedure]

>   This procedure takes the given *str*, converts it into a byte stream using the current
>   locale, and then sends the data to a terminal's printer port. A terminal that has
>   a printer port must terminfo information that describes it, such as *mc5p* or *mc4*
>   capabilities. Explaining this is beyond the scope of this library.
>
>   Those hardware terminal ports and the printers that used them were slow, and the
>   application must take the responsibility to not flood the port.
>
>   The procedure returns `#f` if the write fails. Otherwise, it returns the number of bytes
>   actually printed.

5.2.33 Refresh windows and lines

refresh *win*   [Procedure]

>   The `refresh` routine (or `noutrefresh` and `doupdate`) must be called to get actual
>   output to the terminal, as other routines merely manipulate data structures. The
>   routine `refresh` copies the named window to the physical terminal screen, taking
>   into account what is already there to do optimizations. The `refresh` routine is the
>   same, using `stdscr` as the default window. Unless `leaveok!` has been enabled, the
>   physical cursor of the terminal is left at the location of the cursor for that window.

noutrefresh *win*   [Procedure]

>   Copies the named window *win* to the virtual screen

doupdate   [Procedure]

>   Compares the virtual screen to the physical screen and updates it where necessary.

The `noutrefresh` and `doupdate` routines allow multiple updates with more efficiency
than `refresh` alone. In addition to all the window structures, curses keeps two data structures representing the terminal screen: a physical screen, describing what is actually on the
screen, and a virtual screen, describing what the programmer wants to have on the screen.

The routine `refresh` works by first calling `noutrefresh`, which copies the named window
to the virtual screen, and then calling `doupdate`, which compares the virtual screen to the
physical screen and does the actual update. If the programmer wishes to output several
windows at once, a series of calls to `refresh` results in alternating calls to `noutrefresh` and

doupdate, causing several bursts of output to the screen. By first calling **noutrefresh** for each window, it is then possible to call **doupdate** once, resulting in only one burst of output, with fewer total characters transmitted and less CPU time used. If the *win* argument to **refresh** is the global variable **curscr**, the screen is immediately cleared and repainted from scratch.

The phrase "copies the named window to the virtual screen" above is ambiguous. What actually happens is that all touched (changed) lines in the window are copied to the virtual screen. This affects programs that use overlapping windows; it means that if two windows overlap, you can refresh them in either order and the overlap region will be modified only when it is explicitly changed.

redrawwin *win*   [Procedure]
redrawln *win beg-line num-lines*   [Procedure]
> The **redrawln** routine indicates to curses that some screen lines are corrupted and should be thrown away before anything is written over them. It touches the indicated lines (marking them changed). The routine **redrawwin** touches the entire window.
>
> Returns **#t** on success and **#f** on failure.

5.2.34 Reading and writing a curses screen to a file

scr-dump *filename*   [Procedure]
> The **scr-dump** routine dumps the current contents of the virtual screen to the file *filename*.

scr-restore *filename*   [Procedure]
> The **scr-restore** routine sets the virtual screen to the contents of *filename*, which must have been written using scr-dump. The next call to **doupdate** restores the screen to the way it looked in the dump file.

scr-init *filename*   [Procedure]
> The **scr-init** routine reads in the contents of *filename* and uses them to initialize the curses data structures about what the terminal currently has on its screen. If the data is determined to be valid, curses bases its next update of the screen on this information rather than clearing the screen and starting from scratch. **scr-init** is used after **initscr** or a system call to share the screen with another process which has done a **scr-dump** after its **endwin** call. The data is declared invalid if the terminfo capabilities **rmcup** and **nrrmc** exist; also if the terminal has been written to since the preceding **scr-dump** call.

scr-set *filename*   [Procedure]
> The **scr-set** routine is a combination of **scr-restore** and **scr-init**. It tells the program that the information in *filename* is what is currently on the screen, and also what the program wants on the screen. This can be thought of as a screen inheritance function.

To read (write) the contents of a window from (to) a port, use the **getwin** and **putwin** routines.

All routines return the integer **#f** upon failure and **#t** upon success.

5.2.35 Scroll a window

scroll *win*   [Procedure]

> The `scroll` routine scrolls the window up one line. This involves moving the lines in the window data structure. As an optimization, if the scrolling region of the window is the entire screen, the physical screen may be scrolled at the same time.

scrl *win n*   [Procedure]

> For positive *n*, the `scrl` and `wscrl` routines scroll the window up n lines (line i+n becomes i); otherwise scroll the window down n lines. This involves moving the lines in the window character image structure. The current cursor position is not changed.

> For these functions to work, scrolling must be enabled via `scrollok!`.

> It returns `#f` upon failure, and `#t` upon successful completion.

5.2.36 Terminal attributes

baudrate   [Procedure]

> The `baudrate` routine returns the output speed of the terminal. The number returned is in bits per second, for example 9600, and is an integer. It could return `#f` if this screen is no longer valid.

erasechar   [Procedure]

> The erasechar routine returns the user's current erase character. If the terminal is a dumb terminal and has no erase character, it will return `#f`.

has-ic?   [Procedure]

> The `has-ic?` routine is true if the terminal has insert- and delete- character capabilities.

has-il?   [Procedure]

> The `has-il?` routine is true if the terminal has insert- and delete-line capabilities, or can simulate them using scrolling regions. This might be used to determine if it would be appropriate to turn on physical scrolling using `scrollok!`.

killchar   [Procedure]

> The killchar routine returns the user's current line kill character. If the terminal has no killchar, it will return `#f`.

longname   [Procedure]

> The `longname` routine returns a string that is a verbose description of the current terminal.

termattrs   [Procedure]

> The `termattrs` function return a `logior` of all video attributes supported by the terminal using the standard `A_XXX` constants. The `term-attrs` function is nearly identical, except that it tests rarely used attributes that might someday having to do with wide characters: `A_HORIZONTAL`, `A_LEFT`, `A_LOW`, `A_RIGHT`, `A_TOP`, and `A_VERTICAL`.

termname   [Procedure]

> The `termname` routine returns the terminal name used by `setupterm`.

5.2.37 Refresh routines

touchwin *win*   [Procedure]

touchline *win start count*   [Procedure]

> The `touchwin` and `touchline` routines throw away all optimization information about which parts of the window have been touched, by pretending that the entire window has been drawn on. This is sometimes necessary when using overlapping windows, since a change to one window affects the other window, but the records of which lines have been changed in the other window do not reflect the change. The routine `touchline` only pretends that *count* lines have been changed, beginning with line *start*.

is-linetouched? *win line*   [Procedure]

> Returns `#t` if the specified window and line was modified since the last call to `refresh`.

is-wintouched? *win*   [Procedure]

> Returns `#t` if the specified window was modified since the last call to `refresh>`

untouchwin *win*   [Procedure]

> The `untouchwin` routine marks all lines in the window as unchanged since the last call to `refresh`.

wtouchln *win y n changed*   [Procedure]

> The `wtouchln` routine makes *n* lines in the window, starting at line *y*, look as if they have (*changed*=1) or have not (*changed*=0) been changed since the last call to `refresh`.

5.2.38 Miscellaneous utilities

unctrl *ch*   [Procedure]

> The `unctrl` routine returns a character string which is a printable representation of the character *ch*, ignoring attributes. *ch* is either a simple Guile character or an `xchar`. Control characters are displayed in the `^X` notation. Printing characters are displayed as is.
>
> Compare this to `keyname`.

keyname *ch*   [Procedure]

> The `keyname` routine returns a character string corresponding to the key *ch*. *ch* is either a simple Guile character or an integer key constant like `KEY_HOME`, and can not be an `xchar`. Control characters are displayed in the `^X` notation. Values above 128 are either meta characters, shown in the `M-X` notation, or the names of function keys, or null.

use-env *f*   [Procedure]

> The `use-env` routine, if used, is called before `initscr` or `newterm` are called. When called with `#f` as an argument, the values of lines and columns specified in the terminfo database will be used, even if environment variables `LINES` and `COLUMNS` (used by default) are set, or if curses is running in a window (in which case default behavior would be to use the window size if `LINES` and `COLUMNS` are not set). Note that setting `LINES` or `COLUMNS` overrides the corresponding size which may be obtained from the operating system.

putwin *win output-port*   [Procedure]

> The **putwin** routine writes all data associated with window *win* into an output port, such as a file or string port. This information can be later retrieved using the **getwin** function.
>
> The storage format is binary and is not described.

getwin *input-port*   [Procedure]

> The **getwin** routine reads window related data from an input port. The input port should be backed by a file or string created by **putwin**. The routine then creates and initializes a new window using that data. It returns a new **#<window>**
>
> The storage format is binary and is not described.

delay-output *ms*   [Procedure]

> The **delay-output** routine inserts an *ms* millisecond pause in output. This routine should not be used extensively because padding characters are used rather than a CPU pause.
>
> The return value is unspecified.

flushinp   [Procedure]

> The **flushinp** routine throws away any typeahead that has been typed by the user and has not yet been read by the program.
>
> The return value is unspecified.

curses-version   [Procedure]

> Returns a string that indicates the version of ncurses being used, for example "ncurses 5.9".

%filter   [Procedure]

> This procedure, when called before initscr, restricts the activity of curses to a single line, instead of the to the entire screen.

5.2.39 Window creation

newwin *nlines ncols begin-y begin-x*   [Procedure]

> Calling **newwin** creates and returns a pointer to a new window with the given number of lines and columns. The upper left-hand corner of the window is at line *begin-y*, column *begin-x*. If either *nlines* or *ncols* is zero, they default to (- (lines) begin-y) and (- (cols) begin-x). A new full-screen window is created by calling (newwin 0 0 0 0).

delwin *win*   [Procedure]

> Calling **delwin** deletes the named window, freeing all memory associated with it (it does not actually erase the window's screen image). Subwindows must be deleted before the main window can be deleted.
>
> This function is called implicitly if a window is garbage collected.

mvwin *win y x*   [Procedure]

> Calling **mvwin** moves the window so that the upper left-hand corner is at position *x*, *y*. If the move would cause the window to be off the screen, it is an error and the window is not moved. Moving subwindows is allowed, but should be avoided.

The return value is unspecified;

subwin *orig nlines ncols begin-y begin-x* [Procedure]

Calling **subwin** creates and returns a pointer to a new window with the given number of lines, *nlines*, and columns, *ncols*. The window is at position (*begin-y*, *begin-x*) on the screen. (This position is relative to the screen, and not to the window orig.) The window is made in the middle of the window *orig*, so that changes made to one window will affect both windows. The subwindow shares memory with the window *orig*. When using this routine, it is necessary to call **touchwin** or **touchline** on *orig* before calling **refresh** on the subwindow.

is-subwin? *win* [Procedure]

Returns **#t** if *win* is a subwin. Otherwise, **#f**.

If the underlying ncurses implementation is not capable of reporting whether a window is a subwindow, this function will always return **#t**. This can happen in older versions of ncurses that were compiled with the **NCURSES_OPAQUE** option enabled.

To see if this **is-subwin?** procedure actually works, you can check the constant **%is-subwin-broken**, which will be #f is **is-subwin?** actually works.

derwin *orig nlines ncols begin-y begin-x* [Procedure]

Calling **derwin** is the same as calling **subwin**, except that *begin-y* and *begin-x* are relative to the origin of the window *orig* rather than the screen. There is no difference between the subwindows and the derived windows.

It returns a window that shares memory with *orig*, or **#f** if the window could not be created.

mvderwin *win par-y par-x* [Procedure]

Calling **mvderwin** moves a derived window (or subwindow) inside its parent window. The screen-relative parameters of the window are not changed. This routine is used to display different parts of the parent window at the same physical position on the screen.

The return value is unspecified.

dupwin *win* [Procedure]

Calling **dupwin** returns a new window that is an exact duplicate of the window *win*.

syncup *win* [Procedure]

Calling **syncup** touches all locations in ancestors of *win* that are changed in *win*. If **syncok!** is called with second argument **#t** then **syncup** is called automatically whenever there is a change in the window.

syncok! *win bf* [Procedure]

If **syncok!** is called with the second argument **#t** then **syncup** is called automatically whenever there is a change in the window.

The return value is unspecified.

syncdown *win* [Procedure]

The **syncdown** routine touches each location in *win* that has been touched in any of its ancestor windows. This routine is called by **refresh**, so it should almost never be necessary to call it manually.

cursyncup *win*   [Procedure]

The routine **cursyncup** updates the current cursor position of all the ancestors of the window to reflect the current cursor position of the window.

The return value is unspecified.

5.2.40 Terminal resizing

resizeterm *lines columns*   [Procedure]

The function **resizeterm** resizes the standard and current windows to the specified dimensions *lines* and *columns*. If the windows are increased in size, the extended areas are blank-filled.

It returns **#t** on success or **#f** on failure. It could fail for memory allocation failures or for dimensions that are too small.

5.3 The Function Key Label Library: (ncurses slk)

The **slk** functions in the **(ncurses slk)** library manipulate the set of soft function-key labels that exist on many terminals. For those terminals that do not have soft labels, curses takes over the bottom line of **stdscr**, reducing the size of **stdscr** (and thus the return value of the procedure **lines**). curses standardizes on eight labels of up to eight characters each. In addition to this, the ncurses implementation supports a mode where it simulates 12 labels of up to five characters each. This is most common for today's PC like end-user devices. Please note that ncurses simulates this mode by taking over up to two lines at the bottom of the screen, it doesn't try to use any hardware support for this mode.

This API is definitely in flux.

slk-init *fmt*   [Procedure]

The **slk-init** routine must be called before **initscr** or **newterm** is called. If **initscr** eventually uses a line from **stdscr** to emulate the soft labels, then *fmt* determines how the labels are arranged on the screen. Setting *fmt* to 0 indicates a 3-2-3 arrangement of the labels, 1 indicates a 4-4 arrangement and 2 indicates the PC-like 4-4-4 mode. If **fmt** is set to 3, it is again the PC like 4-4-4 mode, but in addition an index line is generated, helping the user to identify the key numbers easily.

It returns **#t** if *fmt* is a valid value, or **#f** otherwise.

slk-set *labnum label fmt*   [Procedure]

The **slk-set** routine requires *labnum* to be a label number, from 1 to 8 (resp. 12); *label* must be the string to be put on the label, up to eight (resp. five) characters in length. *fmt* is either 0, 1, or 2, indicating whether the label is to be left-justified, centered, or right-justified, respectively, within the label.

The procedure returns **#f** if the terminal or the softkeys were not initialized, or the *labnum* parameter is outside the range of label counts, or if the format parameter is outside the range 0..2, or if memory for the labels cannot be allocated. Otherwise it return **#t**

slk-refresh   [Procedure]
slk-noutrefresh   [Procedure]

These procedure do a **refresh** or **noutrefresh** operation on the slk window.

slk-label *labnum*   [Procedure]

> The **slk-label** routine returns the current label for label number *labnum*, with leading and trailing blanks stripped.

slk-clear   [Procedure]

> This routine clears the soft labels from the screen.

slk-restore   [Procedure]

> This procedure restores the soft labels after an **slk-clear** has been performed.

slk-touch   [Procedure]

> This routine forces all the soft labels to be output next time **slk-noutrefresh** is performed.

slk-attr-on! *attrs*   [Procedure]
slk-attr-off! *attrs*   [Procedure]
slk-attr-set! *attrs color-pair*   [Procedure]
slk-color! *color-pair*   [Procedure]
slk-attr   [Procedure]

> The **slk-attr-on!**, **slk-attr-set!**, and **slk-attr-off!** routines correspond to **attr-on!**, **attr-set!**, **attr-off!**. They have an effect only if soft labels are simulated on the bottom line of the screen. The default highlight for soft keys is **A_STANDOUT**.
>
> The **slk-color!** routine corresponds to **color-set!**. It has an effect only if soft labels are simulated on the bottom line of the screen.
>
> The procedure **slk-attr** returns the attributes and color pair currently set for the soft keys. They are returned as a list of two elements. The first element is a bitmap of attributes; the second element is a color pair number.

5.4 The curses panel library: (ncurses panel)

These are the functions in the (**ncurses panel**) module.

Panels are curses windows with the added feature of depth. Panel functions allow the use of stacked windows and ensure the proper portions of each window and the curses **stdscr** window are hidden or displayed when panels are added, moved, modified or removed. The set of currently visible panels is the stack of panels. The **stdscr** window is beneath all panels, and is not considered part of the stack.

A window is associated with every panel. The panel routines enable you to create, move, hide, and show panels, as well as position a panel at any desired location in the stack.

Panel routines are a functional layer added to curses, make only high-level curses calls, and work anywhere terminfo curses does.

new-panel *win*   [Procedure]

> This procedure allocates a PANEL structure, associates it with *win*, places the panel on the top of the stack (causes it to be displayed above any other panel) and returns the new panel.

update-panels   [Procedure]

   This procedure refreshes the virtual screen to reflect the relations between the panels
   in the stack, but does not call **doupdate** to refresh the physical screen. Use this
   function and not **refresh** or **noutrefresh**. **update-panels** may be called more
   than once before a call to **doupdate**, but **doupdate** is the procedure responsible for
   updating the physical screen.

del-panel *pan*   [Procedure]

   This procedure removes the given panel from the stack and invalidates *pan*

hide-panel *pan*   [Procedure]

   This procedure removes the given panel from the panel stack and thus hides it from
   view. The panel *pan* is not lost, merely removed from the stack.

panel-hidden? *pan*   [Procedure]

   This procedure returns **#t** if the panel is in the panel stack, **#f** if it is not.

show-panel *pan*   [Procedure]

   This procedure makes a hidden panel visible by placing it on top of the panels in the
   panel stack.

top-panel *pan*   [Procedure]

   This procedure puts the given visible panel on top of all panels in the stack.

bottom-panel *pan*   [Procedure]

   This procedure puts the panel at the bottom of all panels.

move-panel *pan starty startx*   [Procedure]

   This procedure moves the given panel window so that its upper-left corner is at *starty*,
   startx. It does not change the position of the panel in the stack. Be sure to use this
   function, not **mvwin**, to move a panel window.

replace-panel! *pan window*   [Procedure]

   This procedure replaces the current window of panel with window (useful, for example
   if you want to resize a panel; It does not change the position of the panel in the stack.

panel-window *panel*   [Procedure]

   Returns the window of a given panel

5.5 The curses menu library: (ncurses menu)

These are the functions in the (**ncurses menu**) module.

5.5.1 Menus Overview

Menu items are individual menu entries. Each menu item has a name – which is the short,
usually single word, description of the item – and a description, which is a longer description
of the menu item. Depending on the format of the menu, the description may or many not
be visible. Each menu item also holds a set of options about the visibility and selectability
of the item.

   A menu is a collection of menu items along with options on how it operates and is
presented.

5.5.2 Menu Item Procedures

new-item *name description* [Procedure]

Returns a new allocated menu item of type with a given *name* and *description*. It can throw an error if the strings are too large or if a memory allocation error occurs.

set-current-item! *menu item* [Procedure]

Given a *menu* and an *item* that has been attached to that menu, this procedure sets *item* to be the current item. It returns an integer that will be one of E_OK, E_BAD_ARGUMENT, E_NOT_CONNECTED if not menu items are attached to this menu, or E_SYSTEM_ERROR.

current-item *menu* [Procedure]

Returns the current item for *menu*.

set-top-row! *menu row* [Procedure]

This procedure sets *menu*'s top row to be *row*. *row* is an integer where zero indicates that the first row is the top row.

This procedure will only have an effect when there are more rows in the menu than are displayed on the screen. If all the menu items can be displayed, this procedure will have no effect and return E_BAD_ARGUMENT.

The number of rows and columns that a menu displays is set by **set-menu-format!**.

It will return one of E_OK, E_BAD_ARGUMENT, E_NOT_CONNECTED if no menu items are attached to this menu, or E_SYSTEM_ERROR.

top-row *menu* [Procedure]

Returns the number of the top menu row being displayed, or **#f** on failure.

item-index *item* [Procedure]

This procedure returns the zero-origin index of this item in its containing menu's item list or **#f** on failure.

item-name *item* [Procedure]

Returns, as a string, the name of the menu item *item*.

item-description *item* [Procedure]

Returns, as a string, the description of the menu item *item*.

set-item-opts! *item opts* [Procedure]
item-opts-on! *item opts* [Procedure]
item-opts-off! *item opts* [Procedure]

These functions set or query the bit mask for *item*. There is only one option bit mask, O_SELECTABLE. When this is on, the item may be selected during menu processing. It defaults to on.

The procedure **set-item-opts** sets the bit mask of *item* to *opts*.

The procedure **menu-opts-on** turns the bits of *opts* on in *item*. The procedure **menu-opts-off** turns off the bits on *opts* in *item*.

These routines will return E_OK on success or E_SYSTEM_ERROR on failure.

`item-opts` *item*   [Procedure]
>   This procedure returns the options bit mask of *item*.

`set-item-value!` *item value*   [Procedure]
`item-value` *item*   [Procedure]
>   If the menu option `O_ONEVALUE` is turned off, the menu can have more than one item selected simultaneously. In this case, the procedure `item-value` can be used to query *item* to see if it is selected. It returns `#t` or `#f`.
>
>   An item can be selected with the procedure `set-item-value!`, which takes a menu item and a boolean *value*. It returns `E_OK`, `E_SYSTEM_ERROR`, or `E_REQUEST_DENIED`.

`item-visible?` *item*   [Procedure]
>   Returns `#t` if *item* is mapped onto the screen. If a menu has more menu items than can be displayed at once, only some of the menu items will be mapped onto the screen.

5.5.3 Menu Procedures

5.5.3.1 Menu Colors and Attributes

`set-menu-fore!` *menu attr*   [Procedure]
`set-menu-back!` *menu attr*   [Procedure]
`set-menu-grey!` *menu attr*   [Procedure]
>   The procedure `set-menu-fore!` sets the colors and attributes of selected menu items. The default is `A_STANDOUT`.
>
>   The procedure `set-menu-back!` sets the colors and attributes of selectable but not currently selected menu items. Its default is `A_NORMAL`.
>
>   The procedure `set-menu-grey!` sets the colors and attributes of unselectable menu items for menus that allow multiple selections. Its default is `A_UNDERLINE`.

`menu-fore` *menu*   [Procedure]
`menu-back` *menu*   [Procedure]
`menu-grey` *menu*   [Procedure]
>   These procedures return the colors and attributes of selected, selectable, and unselectable menu items respectively.

`set-menu-pad` *menu*   [Procedure]
>   This procedure sets the character used to fill the space between the name and the description parts of a menu.

`menu-pad` *menu*   [Procedure]
>   This procedure returns the character used to fill the space between the name and description parts of a menu.

`item-count` *menu*   [Procedure]
>   Returns the number of menu items attached to *menu*.

5.5.3.2 Positioning a menu's cursor

`pos-menu-cursor` *menu*   [Procedure]

> This procedure repositions the cursor the position associated with the menu's current selected item. This is useful if other (non-menu) routines have been called and have moved the cursor away from the menu.

5.5.3.3 The menu driver

`menu-driver` *menu c*   [Procedure]

> Once a menu has been posted (displayed), you should funnel input events to it through menu-driver. This routine has three major input cases:
>
> - The input is a form navigation request. Navigation request codes are constants defined in the table below, which are distinct from the key and character codes returned by `wgetch`.
> - The input is a printable character. Printable characters (which must be positive, less than 256) are checked according to the program's locale settings.
> - The input is the KEY_MOUSE special key associated with an mouse event.
>
> The menu driver request are as follows.

`REQ_LEFT_ITEM`
> Move left to an item.

`REQ_RIGHT_ITEM`
> Move right to an item.

`REQ_UP_ITEM`
> Move up to an item.

`REQ_DOWN_ITEM`
> Move down to an item.

`REQ_SCR_ULINE`
> Scroll up a line.

`REQ_SCR_DLINE`
> Scroll down a line.

`REQ_SCR_DPAGE`
> Scroll down a page.

`REQ_SCR_UPAGE`
> Scroll up a page.

`REQ_FIRST_ITEM`
> Move to the first item.

`REQ_LAST_ITEM`
> Move to the last item.

`REQ_NEXT_ITEM`
> Move to the next item.

REQ_PREV_ITEM

> Move to the previous item.

REQ_TOGGLE_ITEM

> Select/deselect an item.

REQ_CLEAR_PATTERN

> Clear the menu pattern buffer.

REQ_BACK_PATTERN

> Delete the previous character from the pattern buffer.

REQ_NEXT_MATCH

> Move to the next item matching the pattern match.

REQ_PREV_MATCH

> Move to the previous item matching the pattern match.

If the second argument c is a printable character, the code appends it to the pattern buffer and attempts to move to the next item matching the new pattern. If there is no such match, menu-driver returns E_NO_MATCH and deletes the appended character from the buffer.

If the second argument c is one of the above pre-defined requests, the corresponding action is performed.

If the second argument is the KEY_MOUSE special key, the associated mouse event is translated into one of the above pre-defined requests. Currently only clicks in the user window (e.g. inside the menu display area or the decoration window) are handled.

If you click above the display region of the menu:

- a REQ_SCR_ULINE is generated for a single click,
- a REQ_SCR_UPAGE is generated for a double-click and
- a REQ_FIRST_ITEM is generated for a triple-click.

If you click below the display region of the menu:

- a REQ_SCR_DLINE is generated for a single click,
- a REQ_SCR_DPAGE is generated for a double-click and
- a REQ_LAST_ITEM is generated for a triple-click.

If you click at an item inside the display area of the menu:

- the menu cursor is positioned to that item.
- If you double-click an item a REQ_TOGGLE_ITEM is generated and E_UNKNOWN_ COMMAND is returned. This return value makes sense, because a double click usually means that an item-specific action should be returned. It is exactly the purpose of this return value to signal that an application specific command should be executed.
- If a translation into a request was done, menu_driver returns the result of this request.

If you clicked outside the user window or the mouse event could not be translated into a menu request an E_REQUEST_DENIED is returned.

The procedure menu-driver returns one of the following error codes:

`E_OK`   The routine succeeded.

`E_SYSTEM_ERROR`

> System error occurred (see errno).

`E_BAD_ARGUMENT`

> Routine detected an incorrect or out-of-range argument.

`E_BAD_STATE`

> Routine was called from an initialization or termination function.

`E_NOT_POSTED`

> The menu has not been posted.

`E_UNKNOWN_COMMAND`

> The menu driver code saw an unknown request code.

`E_NO_MATCH`

> Character failed to match.

`E_REQUEST_DENIED`

> The menu driver could not process the request.

5.5.3.4 Menu sizes

`set-menu-format!` *menu rows cols*   [Procedure]

> The procedure `set-menu-format!` sets the maximum display size of the given menu.
> If this size is too small to display all menu items, the menu will be made scrollable.
> If this size is larger than the menus subwindow and the subwindow is too small to
> display all menu items, `post-menu` will fail.
>
> The default format is 16 rows, 1 column. A zero row or column argument is interpreted
> as a request not to change the current value.
>
> This procedure returns `E_OK`, `E_SYSTEM_ERROR`, `E_BAD_ARGUMENT` if the routine de-
> tected an incorrect or out-of-range argument, or `E_POSTED` if the menu is already
> posted.

`menu-format`   [Procedure]

> This procedure returns a two-element list containing the display size of the menu in
> rows and columns

5.5.3.5 Menu mark strings

`set-menu-mark!` *menu str*   [Procedure]

> In order to make menu selections visible on older terminals without highlighting or
> color capability, the menu library marks selected items in a menu with a prefix string.
>
> The function `set-menu-mark!` sets the mark string for the given menu. Calling `set-menu-mark!` with a null menu item will abolish the mark string. Note that changing
> the length of the mark string for a menu while the menu is posted is likely to produce
> unhelpful behavior.
>
> The default string is "-" (a dash).

menu-mark *menu*   [Procedure]

> Returns, as a string, the prefix string used by the menu library to designate the selected item.

5.5.4 Menu creation

new-menu *items*   [Procedure]

> Given a list of items, where each item was created by the procedure **new-item**, the procedure **new-menu** returns a menu.
>
> If the menu cannot be created, an error is thrown.

5.5.5 Menu options

set-menu-opts! *menu options*   [Procedure]
menu-opts-on! *menu options*   [Procedure]
menu-opts-off! *menu options*   [Procedure]

> The function **set-menu-opts!** sets all the given menu's option bits (menu option bits may be logically-OR'ed together).
>
> The function **menu-opts-on** turns on the given option bits, and leaves others alone.
>
> The function **menu-opts-off** turns off the given option bits, and leaves others alone.
>
> The following options are defined (all are on by default):
>
> O_ONEVALUE
> > Only one item can be selected for this menu.
>
> O_SHOWDESC
> > Display the item descriptions when the menu is posted.
>
> O_ROWMAJOR
> > Display the menu in row-major order.
>
> O_IGNORECASE
> > Ignore the case when pattern-matching.
>
> O_SHOWMATCH
> > Move the cursor to within the item name while pattern-matching.
>
> O_NONCYCLIC
> > Don't wrap around next-item and previous-item, requests to the other end of the menu.
>
> The procedure will return **E_OK**, **E_SYSTEM_ERROR**, or **E_POSTED** if the menu is already posted.

menu-opts   [Procedure]

> Returns the bitmask of the *menu*'s options.

5.5.5.1 Menu pattern buffer

set-menu-pattern! *menu pattern*   [Procedure]

> Every menu has an associated pattern match buffer. As input events that are printable characters come in, they are appended to this match buffer and tested for a match, as described in **menu-driver**.

The function **set-menu-pattern!** sets the pattern buffer for the given menu and tries to find the first matching item. If it succeeds, that item becomes current; if not, the current item does not change.

It may return the following error codes: **E_OK**, **E_BAD_ARGUMENT**, **E_BAD_STATE** if the outline was called from an initialization or termination function, **E_NO_MATCH** if the character failed to match, or **E_SYSTEM_ERROR**.

menu-pattern *menu* [Procedure]
> The procedure menu-pattern returns the pattern buffer of the given menu.

5.5.5.2 Writing or erasing menus from window

post-menu *menu* [Procedure]
unpost-menu *menu* [Procedure]
> The procedure **post-menu** displays a menu to its associated subwindow. To trigger physical display of the subwindow, use refresh or some equivalent curses routine (the implicit doupdate triggered by an curses input request will do). **post-menu** resets the selection status of all items.
>
> The procedure **unpost-menu** erases menu from its associated subwindow.
>
> These routines return one of the following: **E_OK**, **E_SYSTEM_ERROR**, **E_BAD_ARGUMENT**, **E_POSTED** if the menu has already been posted, **E_BAD_STATE** if the routine was called from an initialization or termination function, **E_NO_ROOM** if the menu is too large for its window, or **E_NOT_POSTED** if the menu has not been posted.

5.5.5.3 Control spacing between menu items

set-menu-spacing! *menu description rows cols* [Procedure]
menu-spacing *menu* [Procedure]
> The procedure **set-menu-spacing!** sets the spacing information for the menu. The parameter *description* controls the number of spaces between an item name and an item description. It must not be larger than **TABSIZE**. The menu system puts in the middle of this spacing area the pad character. The remaining parts are filled with spaces. The parameter *rows* controls the number of rows that are used for an item. It must not be larger than 3. The menu system inserts the blank lines between item rows, these lines will contain the pad character in the appropriate positions. The parameter *cols* controls the number of blanks between columns of items. It must not be larger than **TABSIZE**. A value of 0 for all the spacing values resets them to the default, which is 1 for all of them.
>
> **set-menu-spacing!** will return **E_OK**, **E_POSTED** if the menu is posted, or **E_BAD_ARGUMENT** if one of the spacing values is out of range.
>
> The procedure **menu-spacing** returns the spacing info for the menu as a list of three elements: description, row, and column spacing

5.5.5.4 Associate menus with window

set-menu-win! *menu win* [Procedure]
set-menu-sub! *menu subwin* [Procedure]

```
menu-win menu                                                     [Procedure]
menu-sub menu                                                     [Procedure]
scale-menu menu                                                   [Procedure]
```
> Every menu has an associated pair of curses windows. The menu window displays any title and border associated with the window; the menu subwindow displays the items of the menu that are currently available for selection.
>
> The first four functions get and set those windows. It is not necessary to set either window; by default, the driver code uses `stdscr` for both.
>
> The procedure `scale-menu` returns the minimum size required for the subwindow of menu.
>
> `set-menu-win!` and `set-menu-sub!` will return one of the following, `E_OK`, `E_SYSTEM_ERROR`, `E_BAD_ARGUMENT`, or `E_POSTED` if the menu has already been posted.

5.6 The curses form library: (ncurses form)

These are the functions in the (`ncurses form`) module.

5.6.1 Forms Overview

The form library provides terminal-independent facilities for composing form screens on character-cell terminals. The library includes: field routines, which create and modify form fields; and form routines, which group fields into forms, display forms on the screen, and handle interaction with the user.

5.6.2 Positioning a form window cursor

```
pos-form-cursor form                                             [Procedure]
```
> The function `pos-form-cursor` restores the cursor to the position required for the forms driver to continue processing requests. This is useful after curses routines have been called to do screen-painting in response to a form operation.
>
> It returns `E_OK` if the routine succeeded, `E_BAD_ARGUMENT` if the routine detected an incorrect or out-of-range argument, `E_NOT_POSTED` if the form has not been posted, or `E_SYSTEM_ERROR` if a system error occurred.

5.6.3 Form data

```
data-ahead? form                                                 [Procedure]
data-behind? form                                                [Procedure]
```
> These procedures test if there is ahead or behind the current screen of the given form form. They return `#t` or `#f`.
>
> This could be because a text entry has been declared to have variable size (not O_STATIC) and not all text from the entry is being displayed.

5.6.4 Command-processing loop of the form system

```
%is-form-driver-wide                                             [Constant]
```
> This constant is `#t` if the `form-driver` function is capable of processing characters with representations that are greater than 8 bits.

form-driver *form c*   [Procedure]
Once a form has been posted (displayed), you should funnel input events to it through **form-driver**. This routine has three major input cases:

- The input is a form navigation request. Navigation request codes are constants defined below, which are distinct from the key and character codes returned by **wgetch**.
- The input is a printable character.
- The input is the KEY_MOUSE special key associated with an mouse event.

The form driver requests are as follows:

Name	Description
REQ_NEXT_PAGE	Move to the next page.
REQ_PREV_PAGE	Move to the previous page.
REQ_FIRST_PAGE	Move to the first page.
REQ_LAST_PAGE	Move to the last field.
REQ_NEXT_FIELD	Move to the next field.
REQ_PREV_FIELD	Move to the previous field.
REQ_FIRST_FIELD	Move to the first field.
REQ_LAST_FIELD	Move to the last field.
REQ_SNEXT_FIELD	Move to the sorted next field.
REQ_SPREV_FIELD	Move to the sorted previous field.
REQ_SFIRST_FIELD	Move to the sorted first field.
REQ_SLAST_FIELD	Move to the sorted last field.
REQ_LEFT_FIELD	Move left to a field.
REQ_RIGHT_FIELD	Move right to a field.
REQ_UP_FIELD	Move up to a field.
REQ_DOWN_FIELD	Move down to a field.
REQ_NEXT_CHAR	Move to the next char.
REQ_PREV_CHAR	Move to the previous char.
REQ_NEXT_LINE	Move to the next line.
REQ_PREV_LINE	Move to the previous line.
REQ_NEXT_WORD	Move to the next word.
REQ_PREV_WORD	Move to the previous word.
REQ_BEG_FIELD	Move to the beginning of the field.
REQ_END_FIELD	Move to the end of the field.
REQ_BEG_LINE	Move to the beginning of the line.
REQ_END_LINE	Move to the end of the line.
REQ_LEFT_CHAR	Move left in the field.
REQ_RIGHT_CHAR	Move right in the field.
REQ_UP_CHAR	Move up in the field.
REQ_DOWN_CHAR	Move down in the field.
REQ_NEW_LINE	Insert or overlay a newline.
REQ_INS_CHAR	Insert a blank at the cursor.
REQ_INS_LINE	Insert a blank line at the cursor.
REQ_DEL_CHAR	Delete character at the cursor.

`REQ_DEL_PREV`	Delete character before the cursor.
`REQ_DEL_LINE`	Delete line at the cursor.
`REQ_DEL_WORD`	Delete blank-delimited word at the cursor.
`REQ_CLR_EOL`	Clear to end of line from cursor.
`REQ_CLR_EOF`	Clear to end of field from cursor.
`REQ_CLR_FIELD`	Clear the entire field.
`REQ_OVL_MODE`	Enter overlay mode.
`REQ_INS_MODE`	Enter insert mode.
`REQ_SCR_FLINE`	Scroll the field forward a line.
`REQ_SCR_BLINE`	Scroll the field backward a line.
`REQ_SCR_FPAGE`	Scroll the field forward a page.
`REQ_SCR_BPAGE`	Scroll the field backward a page.
`REQ_SCR_FHPAGE`	Scroll the field forward half a page.
`REQ_SCR_BHPAGE`	Scroll the field backward half a page.
`REQ_SCR_FCHAR`	Scroll the field forward a character.
`REQ_SCR_BCHAR`	Scroll the field backward a character.
`REQ_SCR_HFLINE`	Horizontal scroll the field forward a line.
`REQ_SCR_HBLINE`	Horizontal scroll the field backward a line.
`REQ_SCR_HFHALF`	Horizontal scroll the field forward half a line.
`REQ_SCR_HBHALF`	Horizontal scroll the field backward half a line.
`REQ_VALIDATION`	Validate field.
`REQ_NEXT_CHOICE`	Display next field choice.
`REQ_PREV_CHOICE`	Display previous field choice.

If the second argument is a printable character, the driver places it in the current position in the current field. If it is one of the forms requests listed above, that request is executed.

It is important to note that when characters are Unicode codepoints greater than U+00FF, the form driver will only use them for versions of the wide ncurses form library that are 2014 or newer. For older version of ncurses, only printable characters (which must be positive, less than 256) are allowed. The `%is-form-driver-wide` constant can be used to check if `form-driver` can handle characters whose numerical representations are greater than 256.

If the second argument is the `KEY_MOUSE` special key, the associated mouse event is translated into one of the above pre-defined requests. Currently only clicks in the user window (e.g. inside the form display area or the decoration window) are handled.

If you click above the display region of the form:

- a REQ_PREV_FIELD is generated for a single click,
- a REQ_PREV_PAGE is generated for a double-click and
- a REQ_FIRST_FIELD is generated for a triple-click.

If you click below the display region of the form:

- a REQ_NEXT_FIELD is generated for a single click,
- a REQ_NEXT_PAGE is generated for a double-click and
- a REQ_LAST_FIELD is generated for a triple-click.

If you click at an field inside the display area of the form:

- the form cursor is positioned to that field.
- If you double-click a field, the form cursor is positioned to that field and `E_UNKNOWN_COMMAND` is returned. This return value makes sense, because a double click usually means that an field-specific action should be returned. It is exactly the purpose of this return value to signal that an application specific command should be executed.
- If a translation into a request was done, form_driver returns the result of this request.

If you clicked outside the user window or the mouse event could not be translated into a form request an `E_REQUEST_DENIED` is returned.

If the second argument is neither printable nor one of the above predefined form requests, the driver assumes it is an application-specific command and returns `E_UNKNOWN_COMMAND`. Application-defined commands should be defined relative to `MAX_COMMAND`, the maximum value of these pre-defined requests.

`form-driver` returns one of the following error codes: `E_OK` if the routine succeeded, `E_BAD_ARGUMENT` if the routine detected an incorrect or out-of-range argument, `E_BAD_STATE` if the routine was called from an initialization or termination function, `E_NOT_POSTED` if the form has not been posted, `E_INVALID_FIELD` if the contents of field is invalid, `E_REQUEST_DENIED` if the form driver could not process the request, `E_SYSTEM_ERROR` if a system error occurred, and `E_UNKNOWN_COMMAND` if the form driver code saw an unknown request code.

5.6.5 Making or breaking connections between forms and fields

`set-form-fields` *form fields*   [Procedure]
> This procedure takes a *fields*, which is a scheme list of field types, and assigns them to *form*.
>
> It returns an integer that will have the value `E_OK` on success, `E_BAD_ARGUMENT`, `E_CONNECTED` if the fields are already connected to the form, `E_POSTED` if the form is already posted, or `E_SYSTEM_ERROR` if a system error occurred.

`field-count` *form*   [Procedure]
> Returns the number of fields in `form`.

`move-field` *field row col*   [Procedure]
> This moves the screen position of field to *row*, *col*. The field must not be connected to a form.
>
> It returns an integer that will have the value `E_OK` on success, `E_BAD_ARGUMENT`, `E_CONNECTED` if the fields are already connected to the form, `E_POSTED` if the form is already posted, or `E_SYSTEM_ERROR` if a system error occurred.

5.6.6 Color and attribute control for form fields

`set-field-fore!` *field attr*   [Procedure]
`set-field-back!` *field attr*   [Procedure]
> The procedure `set-field-fore!` sets the attributes of the contents of a field, and `set-field-back!` set the attributes of the unused portion of a field.
>
> They return the constants `E_OK` on success, `E_BAD_ARGUMENT`, or `E_SYSTEM_ERROR`.

`field-fore` *field*   [Procedure]
`field-back` *field*   [Procedure]
> The procedure `field-fore` returns the attributes of the contents of a field, and `field-back` returns the attributes of the unused portion of a field.

`set-field-pad!` *field pad*   [Procedure]
> The procedure `set-field-pad!` sets the character used as blank in the field to the codepoint `pad`.
>
> They return the constants `E_OK` on success, `E_BAD_ARGUMENT`, or `E_SYSTEM_ERROR`.

`field-pad` *field*   [Procedure]
> The procedure `field-pad` returns the codepoint used as the blank in `field`.

5.6.7 Field buffer control

There are functions to set and get the text in a field, as well as to check if that field has been modified.

`set-field-buffer!` *field buf value*   [Procedure]
> The function `set-field-buffer!` sets the numbered buffer of the given field to contain a given string. Buffer 0 is the displayed value of the field; other numbered buffers may be allocated by applications through the *nbuf* argument of `new-field` but are not manipulated by the forms library.

`field-buffer` *field buffer*   [Procedure]
> Returns a string that is the contents of the *field*. *buffer* zero is the visible buffer on the screen. A field may have other buffers if so allocated when the field was created using `new-field`.

`field-status?` *field*   [Procedure]
> The returns the field status of *field*. The field status is set to a non-zero value whenever the field changes.

`set-field-status!` *field status*   [Procedure]
> Sets the field status of *field* to *status*, a boolean.

`set-max-field` *field max*   [Procedure]
> This procedure sets the maximum size for a dynamic field. An argument of zero turns off any maximum size threshold for that field.

5.6.8 Retrieving field characteristics

`field-info` *field*   [Procedure]
> The procedure returns a six-element list of information about the field. The elements of the list are: height, width, row of upper-left corner, column of upper-left corner, number of off-screen rows, and number of working buffers. This information was stored when the field was created, and rows and columns may not be accurate.

`dynamic-field-info` *field*   [Procedure]
> This procedure returns of the actual size of the field and its maximum size as a list. The elements of the list are: rows, column, and max size.

5.6.9 Retrieving field characteristics

set-field-just! *field justification* [Procedure]

This procedure sets the justification attribute of a field to one of `NO_JUSTIFICATION`, `JUSTIFY_RIGHT`, `JUSTIFY_LEFT`, or `JUSTIFY_CENTER`.

field-just *field* [Procedure]

This procedure returns the justification attribute of *field*. It is one of `NO_JUSTIFICATION`, `JUSTIFY_RIGHT`, `JUSTIFY_LEFT`, or `JUSTIFY_CENTER`.

5.6.10 Creating and destroying form fields

new-field *height width toprow leftcol offscreen nbuffers* [Procedure]

The function `new-field` allocates a new field and initializes it from the parameters given: height, width, row of upper-left corner, column of upper-left corner, number off-screen rows, and number of additional working buffers.

dup-field *field toprow leftcol* [Procedure]

The function dup-field duplicates a field at a new location. Most attributes (including current contents, size, validation type, buffer count, growth threshold, justification, foreground, background, pad character, options, and user pointer) are copied. Field status and the field page bit are not copied.

link-field *field toprow leftcol* [Procedure]

This is like **dup-field** except that the new field shares buffers with its parent. Attribute data is separate.

free-field *field* [Procedure]

This explicitly releases the buffer in field, instead of waiting for the garbage collector to take care of it.

5.6.11 Setting and getting field options

set-field-opts! *field opts* [Procedure]
field-opts-on! *field opts* [Procedure]
field-opts-off! *field opts* [Procedure]
field-opts *field* [Procedure]

The function **set-field-opts!** sets all the given field's option bits (field option bits may be logically-OR'ed together).

The function **field-opts-on!** turns on the given option bits, and leaves others alone.

The function **field-opts-off!** turns off the given option bits, and leaves others alone.

The function **field-opts** returns the field's current option bits.

The following options are defined. All are on by default

`O_VISIBLE`

The field is displayed. If this option is off, display of the field is suppressed.

O_ACTIVE   The field is visited during processing. If this option is off, the field will not be reachable by navigation keys. Please notice that an invisible field appears to be inactive also.

O_PUBLIC   The field contents are displayed as data is entered.

O_EDIT   The field can be edited.

O_WRAP   Words that do not fit on a line are wrapped to the next line. Words are blank-separated.

O_BLANK   The field is cleared whenever a character is entered at the first position.

O_AUTOSKIP
            Skip to the next field when this one fills.

O_NULLOK   Allow a blank field.

O_STATIC   Field buffers are fixed to field's original size. Turn this option off to create a dynamic field.

O_PASSOK   Validate field only if modified by user.

5.6.12 Data type validation for fields

These functions set a field to be able to contain only a certain type of input. The user will not be able to move off the field if it contains invalid input.

set-field-type! *field type* ...   [Procedure]
field-type *field*   [Procedure]
    The procedure set-field-type! declares a data type for a given form field. The procedure field-type returns the declared data type. The input *type* is a symbol that is one of the following list. This is the type checked by validation functions. The predefined types are as follows:

TYPE_ALNUM
            Alphanumeric data. Requires a third int argument, a minimum field width.

TYPE_ALPHA
            Character data. Requires a third int argument, a minimum field width.

TYPE_ENUM
            Accept one of a specified set of strings. Requires a third argument pointing to a list of strings; a fourth integer flag argument to enable case-sensitivity; and a fifth int flag argument specifying whether a partial match must be a unique one (if this flag is off, a prefix matches the first of any set of more than one list elements with that prefix). Please notice that the string list is not copied, only a reference to it is stored in the field. So you should avoid using a list that lives in automatic variables on the stack.

TYPE_INTEGER
            Integer data. Requires a third int argument controlling the precision, a fourth long argument constraining minimum value, and a fifth long

constraining maximum value. If the maximum value is less than or equal to the minimum value, the range is simply ignored.

TYPE_NUMERIC

Numeric data (may have a decimal-point part). Requires a third int argument controlling the precision, a fourth double argument con- straining minimum value, and a fifth double constraining maximum value. If your system supports locales, the decimal point character to be used must be the one specified by your locale. If the maximum value is less than or equal to the minimum value, the range is simply ignored.

TYPE_REGEXP

Regular expression data. Requires a regular expression (char *) third argument; the data is valid if the regular expression matches it. Regular expressions are in the format of regcomp and regexec. Please notice that the regular expression must match the whole field. If you have for example an eight character wide field, a regular expression "^[0-9]*$" always means that you have to fill all eight positions with digits. If you want to allow fewer digits, you may use for example "^[0-9]* *$" which is good for trailing spaces (up to an empty field), or "^ *[0-9]* *$" which is good for leading and trailing spaces around the digits.

TYPE_IPV4

An Internet Protocol Version 4 address. This requires no additional argument. It is checked whether or not the buffer has the form a.b.c.d, where a,b,c and d are numbers between 0 and 255. Trailing blanks in the buffer are ignored. The address itself is not validated. Please note that this is an ncurses extension. This field type may not be available in other curses implementations.

5.6.13 Creating forms

new-form *fields*   [Procedure]

Creates a new form given a list that contains fields. The fields are created using new-field.

5.6.14 Form pagination functions

set-new-page *field new-page-flag*   [Procedure]

This procedure sets or resets a flag marking the given field as beginning a new page on its form.

new-page? *field*   [Procedure]

Returns a flag indicating if the given field is the start of a new page on its form.

5.6.15 Setting and getting form options

set-form-opts *form opts*   [Procedure]
form-opts-on! *form opts*   [Procedure]

form-opts-off! *form opts*   [Procedure]

> The function **set-form-opts** sets all the given form's option bits (form option bits may be logically-OR'ed together).
>
> The function **form-opts-on!** turns on the given option bits, and leaves others alone.
>
> The function **form-opts-off!** turns off the given option bits, and leaves others alone.

form-opts *form*   [Procedure]

> This returns the current option bits for the form.

The following options are defined, and all are on by default.

O_NL_OVERLOAD

> Overload the **REQ_NEW_LINE** forms driver request so that calling it at the end of a field goes to the next field.

O_BS_OVERLOAD

> Overload the **REQ_DEL_PREV** forms driver request so that calling it at the beginning of a field goes to the previous field.

5.6.16 Setting the page number and field

set-current-field! *form field*   [Procedure]

> This procedure sets the current field on the form.

field-index *form*   [Procedure]

> This returns the index into the field array that is current for the form.

set-form-page *form n*   [Procedure]

> Sets the page of the form to *n*.

form-page *form*   [Procedure]

> Returns the current form's displayed page number.

5.6.17 Writing or erasing forms from associated subwindows

post-form *form*   [Procedure]

> This procedure displays a form to its associated subwindow. To trigger physical display of the subwindow, use **refresh** or some equivalent routine.

unpost-form *form*   [Procedure]

> This erases the form from its associated subwindow.

5.6.18 Printable form request names

form-request-name *request*   [Procedure]
form-request-by-name *name*   [Procedure]

> These procedures convert a string containing the printable name of a form request to its integer value and vice versa.

5.6.19 Form windows

set-form-win *form win* [Procedure]
form-win *form* [Procedure]
set-form-sub *form sub* [Procedure]
form-sub *form* [Procedure]
scale-form *form* [Procedure]

> Every form has an associated pair of curses windows. The form window displays any title and border associated with the window; the form sub-window displays the items of the form that are currently available for selection.
>
> The first four functions get and set those windows. It is not necessary to set either window; by default, the driver code uses **stdscr** for both.
>
> The function scale-form returns the a list of two elements: minimum size required for the subwindow of form.

Index